"Tim Savage's *Discovering the Good Life* is a [...] begins with one of the most universal of questions: *What is the good life?* Then it answers it by taking us through the Bible, summarizing its whole story through the intercanonical theme of three trees—the tree of the knowledge of good and evil, the tree of life, and the great branch, the shoot from the stump of Jesse—Jesus himself—who took our curse by dying on a tree. This volume is ultimately an apologetic for the Christian life in response to a culture dedicated to seeking personal fulfillment but finding that very thing more and more elusive."

Timothy Keller, Founding Pastor, Redeemer Presbyterian Church, New York City

"With one foot planted firmly in Scripture and the other in culture, Tim Savage unpacks the fullness of life that can be ours right now. If you have ever wondered what 'abundant life' should look like, here is the answer! *Discovering the Good Life* is poetic theology that teaches, refreshes, and, yes, surprises us with all that is available in Christ."

Alistair Begg, Senior Pastor, Parkside Church, Chagrin Falls, Ohio

"So often in our search for satisfaction, we're like treasure hunters wandering without a map. We know what we want—joy, peace, goodness— but we seem to be searching in all the wrong places. In *Discovering the Good Life*, Tim Savage wisely explains the story of Scripture using three trees as guideposts. If you want to experience abundant life, this book faithfully leads you to the treasure of all treasures and the giver of all goodness: Jesus."

Melissa Kruger, Director of Women's Content, The Gospel Coalition; author, *In All Things*

"In *Discovering the Good Life*, Tim Savage addresses the enduring question, *How do we find fullness of life in a world full of trouble?* The answer—as he shows through Scripture, stories, and practical examples—is that Christians who faithfully embrace Jesus Christ will find unbelievable fulfillment by reflecting Christ's indwelling love in all they do. Savage's message will inspire Christians wherever they are in their faith journey."

Jon Kyl, former United States senator (Arizona); former Senate Minority Whip

"*Discovering the Good Life* is an extraordinary book by Tim Savage on how good life can be when Christ is the center of it. Savage always has an eloquent way of teaching the Bible and showing how full our lives can be in Christ. Christian or unbeliever, this book will illustrate how you can be transformed by the unconditional love of Christ."

Carson Palmer, all-pro NFL quarterback; Heisman Trophy winner (2002); first overall pick in the NFL draft (2003)

Discovering the
Good Life

Discovering the Good Life

The Surprising Riches Available in Christ

Tim Savage

:: CROSSWAY®

WHEATON, ILLINOIS

Library of Congress Cataloging-in-Publication Data

Names: Savage, Timothy B., author.
Title: Discovering the good life : the surprising riches available in Christ / Tim Savage.
Description: Wheaton : Crossway, 2019. | Includes bibliographical references and index.
Identifiers: LCCN 2018040999| ISBN 9781433530371 (tp) | ISBN 9781433530395 (mobi) | ISBN 9781433530401 (epub)
Subjects: LCSH: Christian life. | Trees in the Bible.
Classification: LCC BV4501.3 .S2837 2019 | DDC 248.4—dc23
LC record available at https://lccn.loc.gov/2018040999

Crossway is a publishing ministry of Good News Publishers.

LB		29	28	27	26	25	24	23	22	21	20	19
15	14	13	12	11	10	9	8	7	6	5	4	3	2	1

Matt and Jon

Contents

Prologue

This is a book about life.

Life is more than a beating heart and inhaling lungs. It is also an adventure—a search for meaning and satisfaction.

Unfortunately for many people, life can be disheartening, falling somewhere between the merely tolerable and the profoundly disappointing.

But it doesn't have to be that way.

Life can be good, very good. That was certainly the intent of the Creator. When God created life, he meant it to be fulfilling.

How do we find fullness of life in a world full of trouble?

No one ever radiated more life than Jesus Christ. It is the burden of my heart, in the pages that follow, to explore his understanding of life.

First, I want to thank two young men whose lives sprang, many would say, from their mother and me. Yet we know a deeper reality: Matt and Jon are gifts from above. Consistently and by God's grace, they have modeled, and have uplifted our hearts by, the surprising riches of life in Christ.

1

Life, Cynics, and Three Trees

O the glory of that endless life,
   that can at once extend to all Eternity.[1]
Thomas Traherne

What is so good about life?

Our hearts long for a winning answer.

Especially at this electrifying moment of history, when the promise of satisfaction resides at our fingertips, when a single tap of a smartphone can update a wardrobe or tweak a portfolio—especially now, we want to believe that life can be good, really good.

But *is* life good?

Do we awaken each morning with unbridled optimism? Do we greet each day with enthusiasm? Do we revel in the blessing of simply being alive?

To be able to celebrate life without reservation and without regret—that is our greatest desire.

However, most of our celebrating takes place in spite of life, to drown out life's disappointments and to distract from life's demands. The thrill of a fourth-quarter comeback, the anticipation of a beach getaway, the excitement of a cinematic blockbuster—these are the things we celebrate, but usually as diversions from life.

Alexandr Solzhenitsyn, the former Soviet dissident, understood this well. In a commencement address to students at Harvard University in 1978, he chided his youthful audience for their "prescribed smiles and raised glasses" and asked quizzically, "What is all the joy about?"[2] Surely not about life in the late-modern world, where people are restless and mired in discontent.

To the graduates in their mortarboards the Russian sounded unnecessarily glum. They were the starry-eyed Baby Boomers, radical to the bone, overbrimming with confidence, marching for social change with megaphones in hand, and rallying to the cry of a better life. When the rock sextet Rare Earth belted out its lyric, "I just want to celebrate another day of living!" the Boomers cheered wildly, twisted and shouted, and christened the song the anthem of the decade.[3]

Life *must* be celebrated.

But forty years on, we are not so sure.

Searching for Who Knows What

Many now wonder whether Solzhenitsyn, with the corners of his mouth turned downward, had a point. An earlier cynic, the Dutch artist Vincent van Gogh, typifies the uncertainty. His icy relationship with life renders him a modern icon, whose restlessness we applaud. "I'm looking for something all the time."[4]

To be looking for something—that is the popular obsession.

Exactly what we're looking for may not be known, but it doesn't matter. What matters is that we are passionately seeking. In the words of van Gogh, "I am striving. I am seeking. I am in it with all my heart."[5]

In other words, life is more a quest than a discovery, more a journey than an arrival. The British philosopher Bertrand Russell sums it up well: "The search . . . is my entire life . . . the actual spring of life within me."[6]

But we might ask, Isn't a search without a discovery an exercise in futility? Isn't seeking without finding pointless? Who would blame, say, a martian, a cosmic interloper scoping out humanity, for shaking his head in dismay and declaring, "What a peculiar creature is the human being, searching for who knows what and finding not much!"

As citizens of the rising years of the twenty-first century, we fare little better, and it doesn't bode well for finding a happy answer to the question, What is so good about life? Perhaps we ought to concede with the balladeer Joni Mitchell, "I really don't know life at all."[7]

Yet all is not gloom.

Into a milieu every bit as bewildering as our own, into the brooding uncertainty of the first century AD, stepped a teacher who professed to have a winning answer to the question. According to him, life is good, exceptionally good. Almost alone among the philosophers of his day, he depicted life in vibrant hues.

Like the Greek sages before him, he was known by a single name.

Jesus.

Pathway to Abundance

Unusual for a celebrity, Jesus hailed from a backwater village in a barren corner of the eastern Mediterranean. He possessed no academic qualifications. He refused to promote himself by force of personality. And with regard to the social markers of his day—pride, pedigree, and power—he offered no boast.

Yet when Jesus spoke, people listened. In fact, the words he uttered bore such weight that both the angels of heaven and the stones of earth fell silent. What emerged from his lips was divine, the thoughts of God compressed into the tonalities of human speech. And the words were articulations of life, fullness of life.

It is important to note that Jesus did not package his ideas in terms of principles, techniques, or instructions. Rather, he spoke in terms of himself. Uniquely, he pointed to himself as the source of life, as the one in whom true life, good life, could be found.

His message was as succinct as it was compelling.

"I am the life" (John 11:25), Jesus announced triumphantly. And he invited people to find their sustenance in him. "I am the bread of life" (John 6:48).

He promised everlasting benefits. "I am the living bread that came down from heaven. If anyone eats of this bread, he will live forever" (John 6:51).

He guaranteed maximum satisfaction. "I came that they may have life and have it abundantly" (John 10:10).

To audiences weary of life's travails, the words of Jesus must have sounded enormously appealing. Perhaps to some they sounded too good to be true. How could Jesus—how could anyone—offer such bountiful life? How could an itinerant teacher tender more life by far than anyone had before him?

Surely the offer must be pure fantasy, to be rejected out of hand.

But what if it were true?

What if Jesus *does* possess abundance of life?

We must be careful not to dismiss Jesus too quickly. To regard his words as fanciful might be to exhibit a fatal inelasticity of mind. It might be to distance ourselves from the one thing we desire most: satisfaction of life.

An Impressive Record

Certainly, Jesus's track record was impressive. Through the ages, many have dipped their buckets into his well and found refreshment beyond expectation. In celebration of Jesus, master artists have created works of unparalleled beauty—paintings, sculptures, symphonies, prose, and poetry—all celebrating the life discovered in him.[8] In the pages that follow, we will meet many such people, emanating from a variety of times and places, all making the same affirmation: that nothing satisfies such as the life embodied in Jesus.

Why, then, haven't more people tapped into this life? Perhaps even more puzzling, why haven't more Christians tapped into this life, the people who ought to be most receptive?

The answer is simple. Too many people, including too many Christians, labor under the burden of life's disappointments, which invariably distracts from the promises of Jesus. When dreams are dashed and insecurities mount, when relationships implode and illnesses afflict, when failures strike and regrets fester, people can sour on life. Preoccupied by attempts to limit the damage, people neglect the resources available in Jesus.

When even followers of Jesus become sidetracked by disappointment, who remains to venture a good word in celebration of life?

Cast of Cynics

Contemporary social critics do little to uplift our spirits. Specializing in cynicism, authors of literature, pundits in the media, and composers of music—that is to say, the brokers of our modern self-understanding—are prickly interpreters of life.

"We are the hollow men."[9]

"We are blown husks that are finished."[10]

"We see our world . . . [and] the tears roll down."[11]

"Infinite sadness invades our souls."[12]

"The world is turning very dark."[13]

"We gotta get out of this place."[14]

"Life is full of empty promises and broken dreams."[15]

"Life is overrated."[16]

"Life is . . . a battle . . . and mankind [is] generally unhappy."[17]

"Is life even worth living?"[18]

"The sooner [we] jump out the window, the sooner [we'll] find peace."[19]

Doleful assessments such as these depress even the most optimistic among us. We may paste on plastic smiles, but we wonder, secretly, what's the point?

Protest Made and Protest Withdrawn

With every fiber of my being, I want to reject the prevailing skepticism. As I type out these words, I want to protest: "Human life is not inescapably grim. It can be a force for good, for great good."

But before indignation can crystalize in my mind, I am brought back to earth by a blast of cold reality. As a pastor, I encounter much about life that is not good. Rare is the week that I don't face wreckages of human existence. The daughter who, sobbing uncontrollably, leaves a voice message describing the chilling details of her father's suicide; the mother who, decades after aborting her first child, still suffers pangs of guilt and remorse; the CEO who, in the blistering headlines of the morning newspaper, is wrongly accused of mishandling corporate funds; the father who, after months of therapy, realizes that years ago he did sexually abuse his daughter; the college student who, because of an addiction to pornography, fails an important exam and forfeits the dream of postgraduate studies; the parents who, because of a daughter-in-law's insecurity, are denied contact with their only son and endure years of painful separation.

Life is replete with disappointment.

No one is immune.

Every person in the neighborhood, every colleague at work, every player on the team, every classmate at school, every member of church—everyone without exception has or will at some point of his or her life suffer the pangs of loss.

Loss is life's common denominator.

The Beatific Vision

Yet amidst the losses, we still cling to the hope of a life worth celebrating. Many have noted the enduring buoyancy of the human spirit.

The fourth-century churchman Augustine believed that we all yearn for the *summon bonum* (the supreme good).[20] The sixteenth-century playwright William Shakespeare wrote that everyone searches for the "music of the spheres."[21] The seventeenth-century poet Traherne assumed that each person pines for "the invisible and eternal."[22] The eighteenth-century German writer and statesman Johann von Goethe declared that everyone wishes to "jubilate up to the heavens."[23] And the twentieth-century medievalist C. S. Lewis believed that we all seek "to be reunited with something in the universe from which we now feel cut-off."[24]

What does the universal longing for goodness of life suggest except that there must be such a life? According to seventeenth-century philosopher Blaise Pascal, it proves "that there was once in us a true happiness of which all that now remains is the empty print and trace."[25] Rooted in our subconscious is the memory of a life worth celebrating.[26]

But does the memory coordinate with reality?

Is fullness of life possible today?

Nobel laureate Bertrand Russell thinks not. "The center of me is always and eternally a terrible pain, a searching for something beyond what the world contains, something transfigured and infinite, the beatific vision. I don't think it is to be found, but the very thought of it is my life."[27]

Yet what Russell searches for in vain—the beatific vision—Pascal announces in triumph. "What else do our desires proclaim but that there is within each of us an infinite abyss that can be filled only by an infinite and immutable object; in other words, by God himself."[28]

According to Pascal, the desire for fullness of life finds its object in God.

The God of the Bible

Who is God?

Numerous answers fill the book where God's self-disclosure reaches its most noteworthy expression. The book is the Bible. Throughout its pages, we are struck by the compelling nature of God's self-revelation, and also by God's delight in making himself known.

God loves to reveal his glory. For he knows it will redound to our good. He is delighted when we can savor him.[29]

He wants us to "languish no more" and to "be like a watered garden" (Jer. 31:12). He wants "the young women [to] rejoice in the dance, and the young men and the old [to] be merry" (Jer. 31:13).

God is a champion for fullness of life. "I will turn their mourning into joy; I will comfort them, and give them gladness for sorrow. I will feast [their] soul[s] . . . with abundance, and my people shall be satisfied with my goodness" (Jer. 31:13–14).[30]

This is the message of the Bible.

God wants us to thrive. He made us for exceedingly full life.

Unfortunately, too few of us realize it.

As a Christian, I ought to be a specialist in abundance of life. Yet sometimes I become discouraged. I am too easily overcome by life's disappointments. At times, my soul feels empty, my heart parched, and my mind jaded.

It's precisely then that I need an injection of life.

Here is an encouraging word. Despite the difficulties of life, we can never descend to a place beyond the reach of God. Even when we are most disheartened, God can track us down and lift us up.

He can turn on the spigots of refreshment and fill us with abundance of life.

Nowhere is God's pursuit of us more clearly set out than in the biblical story of the three trees. Three very special trees, each of which rewards close examination.

The Three Trees

Trees are symbols of life.

They are nothing if not exquisitely alive.

Trees captivate us by their beauty. From the elegance of a bonsai conifer to the majesty of a coastal redwood, they delight the senses.

Trees also serve us by their utility. They cool us by their shade and warm us by their embers. They supply wood for our homes and pulp for our paper. They cleanse the air we breathe, converting toxins into pure oxygen. They assist us in over five thousand different ways, supplying everything from shoe polish to toothpaste.[31] Most importantly, they provide a reliable source of food, nourishing us with fruits and nuts, sap and roots, bark and leaves.

Without trees our lives would be a pale reflection of what they are now. Without forests and orchards, our lives might vanish altogether.

Not surprisingly, the relationship between trees and human beings is a central theme of the Bible. In the opening stanzas of the Word of God, trees are linked inextricably to life. No sooner does God breathe life into human beings than he fills their garden with a wealth of trees—"every tree that is pleasant to the sight and good for food" (Gen. 2:9).

According to the Holy Scriptures, the history of humanity, from its loftiest attainments to its most crushing defeats, can be comprehended in terms of trees, and especially in terms of three distinct trees.

The Tree of the Knowledge of Good and Evil.

A Shoot from the Stump of Jesse.

The Tree of Life with Its Twelve Kinds of Fruit.

A Riveting Narrative

The storyline of the three trees is filled with tension. It portrays the gift of life as magnificent beyond compare and yet prone to corruption. It depicts human beings as hoisted by dreams of glory and yet humbled by nightmares of despair.

If we want to discover the great blessing of simply being alive, we must unravel this arboreal paradox. We must become students of the three trees.

The narrative of the three trees follows a trajectory that is consistently upward. As we transition from one tree to the next, we move from rags to riches. The first tree reminds us how quickly life can go wrong. The second and the third trees present a pathway to restoration.

The progression from tree to tree resembles the plot of a novel, in which the reader is made to sink in mire at the outset and bathe in glory at the end.

But this is no novel.

The story is not fictional, but true. It traces a path along which each one of us walks. Yet—and here is a sobering word—not everyone is assured of a happy arrival. Not all make it to the third and final tree. The storyline consistently teeters on the brink of ruin. And yet, a steadying Hand is present, directing the script, nudging the narrative to an uplifting conclusion.

Suffice it to say that it is to our advantage to become enmeshed in the storyline of the three trees.

Surprisingly, it is a narrative that escapes the notice of many. It is probably because few think to group the three trees together. We tend to look at the trees individually. We view the first tree—the Tree of the Knowledge of Good and Evil—as a contemptible tree, although we probably ought to venerate it. We look at the second tree—a Shoot from the Stump of Jesse—as an honorable tree, although we probably ought to despise it. And the third tree—the Tree of Life with Its Twelve Kinds of Fruit—well, we hardly know what to do with that one at all.

We must dispel the misconceptions of the three trees. When we comprehend the trees in combination with each other, we shall discover a forest more beautiful than any we have ever entered before, more inspiring than ageless sequoias, more soothing than gentle aspens, more tranquil than island palms.

The three trees—these three only and these three together—restore hope to humanity. They turn valleys into vistas, transform sin into salvation, and instill joy at the simple thought of being alive. They put the word *fullness* back into life.

Here is an invitation you can't resist. Let's venture into the forest together and discover, perhaps for the very first time, just how good life can be.

A word of guidance: each tree must be approached in its appointed order. We must enter the forest at the portal, with the first tree, which is the Tree of the Knowledge of Good and Evil.

2

The Tree of the Knowledge of Good and Evil

I offended in an apple against Him
that gave me the whole world.[1]

Thomas Traherne

As a boy growing up in southern California, I lived among a grove of eucalyptus trees. They were not indigenous trees, but imported from Australia in the late 1800s by the Santa Fe Railroad. The plan was to use the wood as railway ties, to bind together rails for locomotives.

But the people at Santa Fe failed to do their homework. Belatedly it was discovered that the wood of eucalyptus trees was too soft to hold a spike.

The railway's loss was this boy's gain!

Left with acreages of mature trees, I could swing from tree to tree like Tarzan, stopping intermittently at strategically positioned tree forts. It was an enchanted forest, the stuff of every boy's dreams.

Yet it was an accidental bequest, the costly mistake of the executives of the Santa Fe Railroad.

A Fruitful Orchard

When God created the very first forest, he made no mistakes. "'Let the earth sprout with trees bearing fruit,' said God—and it was so" (see Gen. 1:11). Hundreds of trees, perhaps thousands, maybe even millions. The sheer size of the forest must have sparked wonder in the hearts of the original inhabitants. "Behold, I have given you *every* . . . tree" (Gen. 1:29), announced the Creator to his wide-eyed beneficiaries.

Each tree was meant to be a source of delight, both visually—trees "pleasant to the sight"—and nutritionally—trees "good for food" (Gen. 2:9). Moreover, not only did every tree produce its own crop of fruit, but it also bore within itself the capacity to produce additional trees. "God said, 'Behold, I have given you . . . every tree with seed in its fruit'" (Gen. 1:29).

Unlike eucalyptus trees, which tend to sterilize the environment, dropping oily leaves and preventing plants from growing beneath their limbs, the trees of the first garden were spectacularly fertile. They produced fruit in endless supply.

Never would there be a shortage of nourishment in Paradise. Consequently, never would there be a shortage of human satisfaction. Adam and Eve, the initial tenants of Paradise, would always eat to the full.

The lesson of the first orchard is unmistakable: God is a lavish benefactor. He allocates satisfaction in superabundance.

A Boundless Generosity

What an exhilarating picture of the Creator! With hands wide open, tendering gifts of limitless delight to hearts awestruck by his munificence—such is the goodness of God. His generosity knows no bounds.

Too often we cultivate an austere view of God. We think of him as a close-fisted deity, who distributes gifts only sparingly and grudgingly, and reserves the best portions for himself. But the God of the Bible is not a miserly God. He does not hoard for himself. His liberality radiates outward like the rays of the sun, like water gushing from a geyser. He is a self-giving God, constantly pouring himself into creation.[2]

Such outflows of goodness would seem to put a strain on the divine resources. But it is just the opposite: the more God gives of himself, the more he has to give. God appears most full when he is most self-emptying.

A Sinister Allegation

Yet at an early point of history, the generosity of God was put to the test. The devil, in the guise of a serpent, slithered up to the first humans and cast aspersions on the self-giving nature of God. "He said to the woman, 'Did God actually say, "You shall not eat of any tree in the garden"?'" (Gen. 3:1).

The implication is clear: God is withholding something from you. He is refusing to give you every tree of the garden. He is keeping something to himself. He is a self-grasping God.

But the devil was misquoting God. Far from withholding "any" tree of the garden, as the devil insinuated, God had bequeathed a vast plantation of trees. "You may surely eat of *every* tree of the garden" (Gen. 2:16), every tree in a seemingly boundless orchard.[3]

A Valuable Exception

Yet there was an exception.

According to the Lord, one particular tree was off limits. It was the first of our three trees.

"Of the tree of the knowledge of good and evil you shall not eat" (Gen. 2:17).

What could be wrong with withholding a single tree in an unending forest of trees? Apparently enough to impugn God's motives and to accuse him of being a stingy Creator. "The serpent said to the woman, '. . . God knows that when you eat of it your eyes will be opened, and you will be like God, knowing good and evil'" (Gen. 3:4–5). In other words, God doesn't want you to see what he sees and know what he knows. He doesn't want you to be like him. He has withheld the tree just for himself.

There is an element of truth in the devil's claim. God does want to preserve his uniqueness as the one and the only God. But there is also a deception. As we've seen, God lavishes himself on humanity. And nowhere is it more evident than in the gift of the first tree. With the bequest of the Tree of the Knowledge of Good and Evil, God's generosity rises to unimaginable heights.

Seldom do we look at the first tree in this way. Rather, we tend to disparage the Tree of the Knowledge of Good and Evil, regarding it as an intruder in an otherwise pristine paradise, a destructive weed among God's fruitful orchard. After all, it bears within its branches the forbidden fruit, with the power to rain doom on humanity.

Yet there is more to the first tree than meets the eye— so much more that we must rid ourselves of all preconceived notions and focus intently on its God-intended purpose.

Looking carefully at the biblical account, we can see that the first tree is a gift more valuable than the cumulative worth of all the other trees.

A Divine Prohibition

What makes the first tree so special is the prohibition against its fruit. Without such a sanction, the Tree of the Knowledge of Good and Evil would probably differ little from its arboreal neighbors. It would possess leaves, bark, and fruit, just as any other tree. But by declaring it off limits, God distinguishes it from the others, if not by appearance, then at least by function.

How the first tree *functions*—that is what sets it apart.

It plays an important role in the lives of human beings. If they use it well, abstaining from its fruit, they will be blessed. If they misuse it, imbibing its fruit, they will perish.

"In the day that you eat of it you shall surely die," declares the Lord (Gen. 2:17).

The Tree of the Knowledge of Good and Evil has the power either to make or to break human beings.

It holds the key to *life*.

A Walk with God

What exactly is life?

In the beginning, there was no life. But everything changed in one spectacular act. God reversed the barrenness of earth and created humans. "The LORD God formed the man of dust from the ground" (Gen. 2:7).

But there was still no life, just an inert lump of humanity. Not until the Lord "breathed into his nostrils the breath of life [did] the man [become] a living creature" (Gen.2:7). It took an infusion of divine breath to create human life.

God's breath was more than a burst of oxygen jump-starting the lungs. It was holy air, animating the human at the deepest level of his being, filling him with the life of God himself.

The transmission of divine life receives metaphorical depiction in Genesis, above all in the vast orchard itself, which is a symbol of life. "And the LORD God commanded the man, saying, 'You may surely eat of every tree of the garden'" (Gen. 2:16). This is a peculiar command: rarely do humans need to be coaxed into eating their food. But this is more than dinner-table instruction. It is an invitation to *enjoy* the fruit of a limitless expanse of trees, to "eat of *every* tree of the garden." It is a summons to luxuriate in God-given life.

Figuratively, then, the vast forest stands for abundance of life.

But it also stands for more. The metaphor is expanded in Genesis 3, where the man and the woman hear "the sound of the LORD God walking in the garden in the cool of the day" (Gen. 3:8). Here humans discover that God is a perambulating God, walking where they walk among the life-laden trees. In the orchard, Creator and creature come together. What pulsates under the canopy of trees is thus divine life, symbolized both by the fruit-bearing trees and by the presence of God himself.

Mingling with God in the coolness of an orchard, the humans come alive at the core of their beings. Life could not be richer.

Who can measure the goodness of God?

A Holy Love

God's goodness explains God's holiness. Unlike any other god, the God of the Bible empties himself into creation. His generosity sets him apart from all others. It renders him holy.

The Bible has a word for the self-giving nature of God.

It is the word *love*.

According to the apostle John, "God is love" (1 John 4:8). He is love's author, and he is love's exemplar.

In the inaugural garden, God so loved the world that he gave his one and only life—his very own breath and his very own presence.

From earliest times, people have eulogized the love of the biblical God. People such as King David: "You have put more joy in my heart than they have when their grain and wine abound"; "O LORD, our Lord, how majestic is your name in all the earth!"; "You make [me] glad with the joy of your presence"; "Surely goodness and mercy shall follow me all the days of my life"; "Ascribe to the LORD glory"; "Taste and see that the LORD is good!"; "Your steadfast love, O LORD, extends to the heavens"; "As a deer pants for flowing streams, so pants my soul for you, O God"; "Your steadfast love is better than life"; "O LORD, for your steadfast love is good" (Pss. 4:7; 8:1; 21:6; 23:6; 29:1; 34:8; 36:5; 42:1; 63:3; 69:16).

And people such as the apostle Paul: "[God] himself gives to all mankind life and breath and everything"; "God's love has been poured into our hearts"; "We are more than conquerors through him who loved us. . . . [Nothing] in all creation, will be able to separate us from the love of God"; "Because of the great love with which he loved us . . . [God] made us alive"; "Rejoice in the Lord always; again I will say, rejoice!"; "My God will supply every need of yours according to his riches in glory in Christ Jesus. To our God and Father be glory forever and ever" (Acts 17:25; Rom. 5:5; 8:37, 39; Eph. 2:4–5; Phil. 4:4, 19–20).

Outside the Bible, many others pay tribute to the love of God—people such as the Puritans, who are sometimes shunned for severity but who are actually capable of warmhearted praise. Typical is John Owen, the seventeenth-century scholar and chancellor of Oxford University, who expressed sheer delight in the love of God:

> What is more pleasing than the eternal, free, and fruitful *love* of the Father? Sit down at this fountain and you will quickly discover the sweetness of its streams. Instead of running from God, you will not be able to remain at a distance any longer.[4]

This ought to be our testimony as well. We, too, can sit down at the fountain of God's love and bask in its sweet delights.

A while ago, I leaned back and crossed my legs on the top of a bluff overlooking the Pacific Ocean. The sun, sinking in the evening sky, painted the sea in shades of silver and gold, showcasing a dazzling array of currents, diagonal lines shimmering this way and that. Soon a school of dolphins rose to the surface and began to ride the waves, twisting and tumbling, frolicking in the surf. Then a pelican swooped into the frame and glided with ease inches above the waves, dropping its beak into the water to scoop up small fish in a display of remarkable dexterity. Finally, a silhouette came into view, a more distant, geometric shape, a quivering triangle, the majestic sail of a schooner returning to harbor.

When at last the sun gave up the day, disappearing into a ball of flaming orange, the sea turned from gold to cobalt blue and finally to steely black. Only the sound of the breakers and the sight of the moon remained, promising a repeat performance in the morning.

The grandeur I witnessed from the bluff was not dissimilar to the charms of the succulent orchard, and a powerful reminder of God's many gifts to us. Daily, we can sit down at the fountain of creation and consume the sweetness of God's love.

A Love Returned

The love of God calls for a response. It invites a return.

That is because love is always interpersonal, flowing from one person to another and back again.

As recipients of God's love, we are encouraged to complete the circle of love, to return God's love with a reciprocal love.

Yet how can finite beings reciprocate God's love?

His love is infinite. His love is perfect. To return a measureless and an unblemished love requires something equally unique.

We are incapable of love in these dimensions.[5]

It is precisely at this point that the first tree proves its inestimable worth. It enables us to return to God an appropriate love. And it does so—surprisingly—by providing an alternative to loving God.

An Option

The Tree of the Knowledge of Good and Evil presents us with an option. We can either refuse its fruit or eat its fruit. If we refuse, we show ourselves obedient to God. If we eat, we show ourselves disobedient.

But there is more to the option than obeying and disobeying. At a deeper level, we are opting either to return God's love or to spurn it, either to complete the circle of love or to break it.

This is a pivotal insight.

By rejecting the fruit of the first tree, humans express satisfaction with God, with the abundance of his orchard, and with the gift of his life. By eating from the first tree, they exhibit dissatisfaction with God, with his orchard, and with his life.

To put it another way, by opting for the orchard, humans return God's love. By opting for the forbidden fruit, they reject it.

An Exclusive Love

It is not unlike what happens in marriage. At a wedding, husbands and wives exchange vows. They pledge to unite themselves to each other and to forsake all others. They promise an *exclusive* love. "I will love you *and no one else.*"

Starry-eyed romantics are happy to make this vow. Frequently, they whisper little ditties into each other's ears. "You are mine and mine *alone!*" "*Only* you hold the key to my heart!" "I can't see myself with anybody *else!*" They promise themselves to each other and to each other *alone.*

It is precisely the exclusivity of the promise that cements their bond.

In our relationship with God, we forge a similar bond. We pledge ourselves to him and to him *alone.* Regardless of how enticing other gods may be, we promise to love God and God *only.*

"There is none like you among the gods, O Lord" (Ps. 86:8), avows King David.[6]

Exclusive vows sometimes feel constricting, since they close the door to other options, and yet they can actually be liberating.

When I stood in front of the altar and vowed to my beautiful bride, Lesli, to love her and her *alone*, I did not regret what I was giving up. I did not rue the doors I was shutting or the limitations I was imposing on myself. On the contrary, I celebrated the wonder of what was opening up before me, a circle of love in which the two people, Lesli and I, would give *all* of ourselves to the other and to the other *exclusively.*

It is important to note that every circle of love contains a negative ingredient, namely, a pledge *not* to give one's love to another. In order to give an exclusive "Yes" to Lesli, I needed to give an emphatic "No" to others.

It is the same in our relationship with God. To complete the circle of love with our Maker, we must pledge ourselves to him and to him *alone*.

An Authentic Pledge

Here it is important to note that the exclusive nature of our vow requires at least some knowledge of what we are giving up. We must be aware (to some degree) of the gods to whom we are not binding ourselves in love.

It is exactly this awareness that the first tree provides. By standing over against the other trees, it presents an alternative to the life offered by God. It gives humans an option, an apparent second path to life. By providing an alternative, it thus makes a genuine pledge to God possible.[7]

For this reason, the Tree of the Knowledge of Good and Evil is a priceless bequest. It enables humans to seal a loving relationship with their Maker. It helps to cement their union with him.

A Complete Satisfaction

But it does something else as well, something perhaps even more valuable. It enables humans to affirm *complete* satisfaction with God.

Without the first tree, they are able only to affirm *partial* satisfaction. In order to express *full* satisfaction they need to be aware of alternative paths to satisfaction. The first tree provides that awareness.

By rejecting its fruit, Adam and Eve affirm that God is *enough* for them. In him, they find *entire* satisfaction.

We can now see why the gift of the first tree is such a strategic bequest. By its presence in the garden of Eden, humans are able both to complete the circle of love, returning an exclusive love to their Maker, and to express complete satisfaction with God, acknowledging that he is enough for them.

Through the first tree they can affirm that life in God is incomparably good and comprehensively satisfying.

A Love Neglected

But the affirmation is short-lived. As beneficiaries of the superabundant life of God, the first humans fail to sustain fullthroated praise. Instead, they take life for granted and, shortly thereafter, become very unalive.

In the novel *Crime and Punishment*, the Russian author Fyodor Dostoevsky illustrates the point through a heroine named Sonya. She is the daughter of a man who wastes his wages on alcohol, and of a woman who is so browbeaten that she can rarely pull herself out of bed, and the older sister of a girl whose food depends on the income Sonya feels compelled to earn in the beds of lecherous men.

Sonya sacrifices herself, all of herself, for her family.

She also gives herself to a cold-blooded murderer by the name of Raskolnikov. Humbly, she pledges to "live only in his life."[8] But Raskolnikov takes advantage of Sonya and responds to her love with cruelty.

How could Raskolnikov spurn a love so great?

Yet—and here is the point of Dostoevsky—we all spurn such love. We neglect a love far greater than that of the selfgiving Sonya. We take for granted the gift of God's love. We don't respond to his love by pursuing life in him and in him *alone*.

Perhaps we are unaware of the vast dimensions of God's love.

According to the Holy Scriptures, the love of God extends to the heavens[9] and endures forever.[10] It is slow to anger and full of mercy and grace.[11] It bears no grudges, requires no payments, plays no games, asks no favors, seeks no advantages, and demands no benefits.[12]

The love of God is unexampled in magnitude and beauty.

Had Adam and Eve enmeshed themselves in this love, they would have lived happily ever after. But as we know, they fell prey to the deceptions of a serpent. They allowed the devil to entice them with the fruit of the first tree.

"When the woman saw that the tree [of the Knowledge of Good and Evil] was good for food, and that it was a delight to the eyes, and that the tree was to be desired to make one wise, she took of its fruit and ate, and she also gave some to her husband who was with her, and he ate" (Gen. 3:6).

It was a catastrophic bite, dooming the first humans, as well as their progeny, as well as all of us.

Everything that ails humanity can be traced to that fateful decision.

Why did Adam and Eve eat the forbidden fruit?

The Tyranny of Desire

The answer can be summed up in one word: *desire*. Powerful and passionate desire.

"Desire," claims the Dutch philosopher Spinoza, "is the very essence of a man."[13]

"What is man without desires?" asks Dostoevsky.[14]

To know what a person desires is to know who a person is. People are nothing except the summation of their desires.

Desire rouses us from bed in the morning. Desire fuels our movements during the day. Desire seeks promotion at work. Desire pursues contentment at home. Desire yearns for warmth in relationships. Desire shapes ambitions. Desire dictates choices.

Desire—always profound, rarely indifferent, perpetually insistent—is the engine that drives humanity.[15]

Desire Unfulfilled

But desire can be vexing.

Seldom is desire satisfied. Rarely does it come to an end. Always it begets more desire.

Take, for example, the desire for money. When riches abound, desire does not vanish. Rather, it morphs into new desire, perhaps for more money, or perhaps for something else altogether.

Ralph Waldo Emerson was right when he observed: "Much will have more!"[16]

It is an aphorism comprehended well by John D. Rockefeller, who, in the early twentieth century, was the world's richest human, cornering a whopping 30 percent of the GNP of the United States of America. However, shortly before his death, he confessed: "I have made millions but they have brought me no happiness."[17]

A well-heeled railway baron of the same era, John Jacob Astor, expressed even greater dismay: "I am the most miserable man on earth."[18]

Another railway tycoon, Andrew Carnegie, lamented: "Millionaires seldom smile!"[19]

Startup founder Markus Persson, who sold Minecraft to Microsoft for $2.5 billion and bought a $70 million mansion, complained: "I've never felt more isolated."[20]

Money, even exorbitant sums of it, fails to satisfy desire.[21] Nor does anything else: prestige, popularity, or power.

Jerry West is a member of the National Basketball Association Hall of Fame, winner of NBA championships both as a player and as a general manager, and the person whose silhouette adorns the logo of his sport. Despite his many successes, West suffers from melancholy. "As far as I'm concerned, I haven't done anything. . . . Even though I sometimes feel, 'My goodness, you're among the upper echelon,' there is still a huge void there. A huge void."[22]

Michael Phelps, the most decorated Olympian of all time, accumulated a remarkable twenty-eight medals. Yet amidst fame and success, he was disconsolate. "I thought the world would just be better off without me. I figured that was the best thing to do—just end my life."[23]

Regardless of attainments, we never attain enough. Desire sees to it.

The American novelist, John Cheever, concludes: "The main emotion of the adult American who has all the advantages of wealth, education, and culture is disappointment."[24]

Colossal achievement, chronic disappointment!

Mark Twain was right: "We don't know quite what it is we do want, but it just fairly makes our heart ache we want it so."[25]

When was the last time you heard a friend or a colleague or a relative exclaim triumphantly, "I have everything I want! I am satisfied! I desire nothing else!"

On the contrary, unrelenting desire is every person's torment.

While this may confound us, it does not confound God. He created us, and he created us with desire. He made us with *mammoth* desire. And he did so for a purpose, a purpose encapsulated in the Tree of the Knowledge of Good and Evil.

When the devil coiled himself in its branches, he zeroed in on human desire—the desires of hunger, pleasure, and wisdom. Beguilingly, he tempted his human prey: "The tree [is] good for food, and . . . a delight to the eyes, and . . . to make one wise" (Gen. 3:6).

Eat, and your desires will be fulfilled.

It was a lie.

Far from assuaging desire, the fruit of the first tree awakened despair. And it prompted expulsion from the succulent orchard.

"The Lord God sent [them] out from the garden of Eden" (Gen. 3:23).

Chasing desire, the first humans lost Paradise.

This is the lesson of the first tree, and it is a lesson we ignore at our peril.

When we seek to satisfy our desires apart from God, we will not find satisfaction of life; instead, we will find a life greatly diminished.

So what do we do with desire? Do we regard it as a cruel trick, causing us to yearn for what can never be found?

Desire Fulfilled

When nothing on earth satisfies, where do we look?

We look beyond earth.

We look to God, which is precisely what God intended. He created us with desires so big that they could be fulfilled only in him.[26]

In a classic statement, C. S. Lewis wrote:

> Creatures are not born with desires unless satisfaction for those desires exists. A baby feels hunger: well, there is such a thing as food. A duckling wants to swim: well, there is

such a thing as water. Men feel sexual desire: well, there is such a thing as sex. If I find in myself a desire which no experience in this world can satisfy, the most probable explanation is that I was made for another world.[27]

Traherne agrees: "My desires [are] so august and insatiable that nothing less than a Deity [can] satisfy them."[28]

God-given desire points away from earthly things to something higher, indeed, to God himself.

Desire, then, is not a cruel trick (luring us with false hopes), or a malign impulse (steering us to destructive ends), or a recipe for despair (afflicting us with disappointment). On the contrary, desire drives us home.[29]

More of or More Than?

This is the great benefaction of the Tree of the Knowledge of Good and Evil. It points us to the true object of our desires. Indeed, it poses an implicit question: Will you seek your fulfillment in the heavenly Father, or will you seek it in the things of earth?

Or to put it another way, will you seek fulfillment in more *of* what God gives you in himself—more *of* his love, more *of* his goodness, more *of* his joy, more *of* his power, more *of* his truth—or will you seek fulfillment in more *than* what God gives you in himself?

More *of* God or more *than* God?

Unhappily for the first humans, it was the latter. Falling under the spell of the serpent, they grasped for life in more *than* what they received in God.[30]

Their blunder has become every person's downfall. Men and women of every stripe, nation, and era have fallen prey to the temptation to seek satisfaction apart from God.

None is exempt.

If we are honest, we can acknowledge this from personal experience. We have all looked for satisfaction in earthly things: romance, popularity, self-respect, work, success, power, wealth, influence, education, entertainment, promotions, homes, retirement, children, and any number of other possibilities in an endless chain of options. Nothing in the chain is essentially bad; in fact much is positively good. But none can ultimately satisfy the human heart.

To look for life in more *than* what God offers in himself is to court disappointment.

For the first humans, it was colossal disappointment. It was condemnation to death—not in the sense that their hearts stopped beating and their lungs stopped inhaling, not physical death (although that, too, would follow), but in the sense that they were cut off from fullness of life. They were separated from the source of life, from their Creator. They were banished from the garden of God.

It was a separation more painful than physical death. Still standing, still breathing, still searching, and yet severed from the life for which they were created.[31]

They were the walking dead.[32]

An Ugly Word or a Good Word?

There is a word in the Bible for seeking to build a life apart from God.

It is the word *sin*.

Sin is an ugly word. If we had our way, we would probably banish it from our vocabulary, regarding it as a useless relic of a religious past. But banish it we must not. Sin is actually a good word, for it discloses the root of our problem. Without an understanding of sin, we don't know what ails us and, consequently, how to seek a cure.

According to the apostle Paul, "All have sinned and fall short of the glory of God" (Rom. 3:23). Everyone has, at some point or other in his or her life, looked for satisfaction in more *than* what is found in God alone.

Everyone is guilty of sin.

And sin exacts a penalty: "The wages of sin is death" (Rom. 6:23).

As a boy, I was terrified by the penalty. The wages of sin . . . death? Sin . . . a capital crime? What could be more horrible? Lying awake at night, I would squirm in my bed and shudder at the harshness of it all.

Adam and Eve would hardly know what hit them. One munch on a piece of fruit and it was all over—separated from God, dispossessed of life, inducted into The Walking Dead Club.

I wouldn't wish such condemnation on my worst enemy. And I certainly wouldn't wish it on myself.

In time, however, my thinking began to change. What seemed in childhood a horrifying penalty became in my teens a sensible judgment.

I started to see things God's way.

A Shameless Rebellion

When the first humans ate from the Tree of the Knowledge of Good and Evil, they did more than ingest a piece of fruit. They attempted to build a life apart from God. They sought more in life *than* what they received in him. Put bluntly, they mounted an assault on the Creator. They attempted to grasp on their own what could be given only by God.

It was a shameless power play. Attempting to usurp the position of the Creator, they effectively made themselves out to be God.

"Then the LORD God said, 'Behold the man has become like one of us'" (Gen. 3:22).[33]

God could not permit such an insurrection. To tolerate rivals to his throne would be to imperil his own "god-ness," as the one and the only God. By definition, God could not allow pretenders to his deity.[34]

He had to put an end to sin before sin (at least conceptually) put an end to him.

Not without reason, the wages of sin *must* be death.

A Gracious Explanation

Still to many of us, it seems like an excessive penalty.

Gratefully, the Lord understands our unease and goes to lengths to explain why sin merits death. Drawing an analogy from marriage, he casts himself as the doting husband and us as his beloved bride. It is an analogy found throughout the Bible, but appears perhaps most poignantly in the writings of the prophet Ezekiel:

> "When . . . you were at the age for love, . . . I made my vow to you and entered into a covenant with you, declares the LORD GOD, and you became mine. Then I bathed you with water . . . and anointed you with oil. I clothed you also with embroidered cloth and shod you with fine leather. I wrapped you in fine linen and covered you with silk. And I adorned you with ornaments and put bracelets on your wrists and a chain on your neck. And I put . . . earrings in your ears and a beautiful crown on your head. . . . Your renown went forth among the nations because of your beauty, for it was perfect through the splendor that

I had bestowed on you, declares the LORD God." (Ezek. 16:8–14)

The Lord heaps every kind of goodness on his young bride, adorning her with silk, bracelets, earrings, and a crown. He withholds nothing. He makes her queen of his life, heiress to his treasure.

And he does the same to us.

As an indulgent spouse, he pampers us with all good things. He blesses us by his presence. He satisfies us with his life.

"I am the LORD your God . . . open your mouth wide, and I will fill it" (Ps. 81:10).

Such love invites a return, the very best return we can make.

Yet according to Ezekiel, we respond with indifference. We turn away from God and seek to make a life of our own. We throw ourselves at other would-be lovers, passersby who tempt us with various allurements.

"[You] played the whore . . . and lavished your whorings on any passerby" (Ezek. 16:15).

How can we, so blessed by the riches of God, hurl ourselves at others? How can we exchange the life of God for pale counterfeits? How can we lie down in the beds of imposters?

Anger Aroused

Perhaps even more significant is the question: How will God respond to our infidelities?

According to Ezekiel, he will respond in the only way a good husband can respond when his bride takes his gifts but refuses his embrace, assumes his name but rejects his companionship, delights in his wealth but defiles his bed.

He responds in white-hot anger.

To respond in any other way would be to make a mockery of his love.

Godly anger is the flip side of godly love. Not to be angry in the face of unfaithfulness is not truly to love.

Even so, God refuses to abandon us. He may let us go—for he will never impose himself on us—but he will not reject us. He never forgets his wedding vows.

Still, he treats our infidelities with the gravity they deserve.

In the case of Adam and Eve, it meant removal from the garden.

"Therefore the LORD God sent [them] out from the garden of Eden . . . and . . . placed . . . a flaming sword that turned every way to guard the way to the tree of life" (Gen. 3:23–24).

God sealed off Paradise.

But even this was an act of compassion. Love protects what is holy. To allow sin to besmirch Eden would be to defile love.[35]

Paradise Lost

So, is Paradise off-limits?

It is for people who seek more in life *than* what God offers in himself. The flaming sword, rotating this way and that, sees to it.

Must we remain forever on the outside looking in?

If the condition of our world is any indication, the answer would seem to be an unqualified yes.

Very little in the world resembles Paradise.

We have recently emerged from history's bloodiest century, the twentieth, and have not yet learned its lessons.[36] We are now embroiled in the birth pangs of a new century, the twenty-first, in which wars continue to rage in over forty countries, churning out parentless children, raped bodies, and withered hearts.

The Tree of the Knowledge of Good and Evil   47

While most of us are able to escape wounds to the body, few of us avoid injuries to the soul. Psychological trauma—the consequence of stormy relationships, gnawing guilt, painful failures, and dogged addictions—afflicts most of us. Even those in the lucky minority, those who manage to escape the worst of the psychological trauma, succumb to common griefs such as loneliness, fear, and despair. At one point or other, we all succumb to a biting word, a cold shoulder, or a caustic rebuke.

Clearly, none of us resides in Paradise.

A cinematic heroine recently gave vent to the contemporary angst: "I'm tired of being dead, and I want to come back to life."[37]

Paradise is a fading memory, and we now know why. The first tree tells us why. By attempting to make a life for ourselves apart from God, we have orchestrated our own downfall. Instead of walking with our Maker in the cool of the day, we have relegated ourselves to an infernal wasteland.

Curse or Blessing?

Curses, then, to the Tree of the Knowledge of Good and Evil. It is the cause of so much grief.[38]

Actually, no.

The first tree is a great blessing. Amidst the chaos, it points the way to fullness of life. It is the only thing that does. It points us to more *of* what God gives us in himself. It invites us into the circle of God's love.

Blessed tree!

Even so, isn't it a mistitled tree?

Surely it ought to receive a more abbreviated name: the Tree of the Knowledge *of Good*. For it points the way to goodness of life.

Perhaps God would have so named it had it not been for his love. Love demands the addition of the phrase *and Evil*. For without evil, without the option to pursue life apart from God, humans could never register entire satisfaction with God, and hence could not enter the circle of his love.

By opening a window to the possibility of his own rejection, God opened a door to a truly loving relationship with him. In the unsearchable riches of the counsels of heaven and from the bottomless reaches of his own love, God conceived a purpose even for evil.[39]

Thus Traherne: "O Thou who wouldst never have permitted sin, hadst Thou not known how to bring good out of evil."[40]

Praise God for the Tree of the Knowledge of Good *and Evil*. Although it remains an incomplete tree, unable by itself to deliver fullness of life, it does point the way.

God Is Life

Russian author Leo Tolstoy understood this well. In his autobiography, he provides an assessment of his own search for life.

> I had a kind, loving and beloved wife, lovely children, and a large estate that was growing and expanding with no effort on my part. I was respected by relatives and friends. I was praised by strangers and could consider myself a celebrity without deceiving myself. Moreover I was not unhealthy in mind or body, but on the contrary enjoyed strength such as I had rarely witnessed in my contemporaries.[41]

Tolstoy had it all—family, wealth, reputation, and health. His every earthly desire was fulfilled. Yet the Count of Yasnaya Polyana was inconsolable. "In these circumstances I found myself at a point where I could no longer go on living, since I feared death."[42]

Death terrified Tolstoy because, at its arrival, it would dispossess him of everything—relationships, achievements, possessions. The fruit of his labor would vanish in an instant.

Death would make a mockery of his life.

Unable to find satisfaction under the sun, Tolstoy looked upward.

"I began to search for God."[43]

When Tolstoy found God, he found life. "To know God and to live are one and the same thing." To which he added triumphantly: *"God is life."*[44]

This is the lesson of the Tree of the Knowledge of Good and Evil. In the God of the Bible alone can fullness of life be found.

Open-Mindedness or Narrow-Mindedness

Many people today reject the lesson. It sounds too narrow-minded. Late-modernity believes there are many paths to life. To insist on one path in particular is unnecessary and objectionable.

Yet it would be patently wrong to accuse the God of the Bible of being narrow-minded. He is actually exceedingly broad-minded. He is unbounded in every way (Pss. 90:1–2; 147:5; Isa. 40:28; Rev. 1:8).

His love is deeper than the ocean (Pss. 36:5; 65:4–7; 146:5–6). His purposes are wider than the galaxies (Ps. 103:11; Isa. 55:8–9). His righteousness is higher than the heavens (Job 11:7–8; Isa. 55:9; Eph. 4:10). His glory is more dazzling than the sun (Isa. 30:26; 60:19; Rev. 21:23).

It takes an open mind—indeed, an enormously expansive mind—to countenance a God of such dimensions.

Moments after typing these words I received a phone call from our son in New Hampshire. He wanted to relate a recent conversation with his professor at Dartmouth College. While discussing major religions, our son expressed esteem for the God of the Bible. It earned a quick rebuke from the professor, who warned him against narrow-mindedness. "If you accept what the Bible says, you'll dismiss alternative views. That would be intolerant. You must maintain an open mind."[45]

In reply, our son suggested that, in his experience, open minds often gravitate to the God of the Bible. It takes broad-mindedness to accept a Creator whose works are supernatural and whose love is infinite.

Ironically—at the other end of the spectrum—late-moderns also espouse a rigid closed-mindedness. You see it, for example, on public highways. Posted alongside roads are exclusive truth-claims such as "Wrong Way," "Dead End," and "Merging Traffic." Few drivers object to the apparent intolerance. Instead, they salute the department of motor vehicles for preserving public safety. Narrow-mindedness is a commendable trait when it saves lives.

Fending Off Death and Enriching Life

A few years back, I set out to climb to the top of Mount Tekarra in the Canadian Rockies. Seasoned trekkers warned me that it would be a demanding ascent and that only one route would convey me safely to the summit. Every other path, they cautioned, could prove fatal. Narrow advice to be sure, but spoken by people who intended me good. I listened to them as though my life depended on it.

True to their word, the climb was perilous, with only a narrow ridge delivering me securely to the top. I had to negotiate the last pitch on all fours, crawling over wet shale, for every two feet forward slipping one foot backwards.

Arriving at the summit, I was rewarded by a spectacular panorama: range after range of sparkling peaks, massive glaciers, tumbling waterfalls, verdant valleys, mountain goats skipping among granite ledges, and alpine moss sprouting fragrantly at my feet. It seemed like a prelude to heaven itself. Yet—and here is the point—I would have missed all the splendor had I not heeded narrow advice.

"There's only one safe route to the summit. All others could prove fatal."

Narrow prescriptions can both fend off death and enrich life.

Losing Our Way

It is tempting to climb the mountains of our existence without God. But we must resist. Otherwise, we shut the door to Paradise and invite hazardous missteps.

Yet admittedly, we all stray from God's path. At one point or other, we all lose our way. And when we wander off, it is difficult to find the way back to God.

The good news is that God can find his way to us.

Having reached down with the gift of the first tree, he can reach down again with the gift of a second tree. What the first tree could not do—deliver us safely to the summit of life—the second tree can.

Are we ready for the second tree?

First, we must confess our need of it, acknowledging that we have veered from the trail. We must admit our sin.

Second, we must ask—we must pray—that God would reach down to us again with a second tree.

The Lesson of the First Tree

Long ago, God reached down to a man named Saul.

Saul was born into privilege, a member of the most respected clan of his nation. He was well educated, a student of the most renowned scholar of his day. He was climbing the ladder of social respectability faster than any of his contemporaries (Gal. 1:14).

Saul's every earthly desire was satisfied.

Yet something was missing.[46]

One day, en route to a neighboring city, Saul was confronted by a heavenly light. It was a light so bright that it knocked him to the ground.

A voice called out from the light and asked Saul to give an account of himself. "Saul, Saul, why are you persecuting me?"

Saul knew it was God. No one else could appear in such splendor. Trembling, he responded, "Who are you Lord?"

The voice replied: "I am Jesus, whom you are persecuting" (Acts 9:4–5).

Saul had been tormenting a group of people on the eastern edge of the Mediterranean who were followers of a teacher named Jesus. Confronted by the heavenly voice, Saul realized the error of his ways. The Jesus he had been opposing was in fact the Lord of glory.

Immediately, Saul was awakened to the lesson of the first tree, and he confessed the error of his ways. He repented. He turned around. He entrusted his life to Jesus.

And Jesus received him, reaching down and lifting him up, and leading him down a path appointed specifically for him. It was a path leading to the second tree.

By the time Saul arrived at the second tree, he had another name.

By the time he arrived at yet another tree, the third tree, he had a new heart.

Saul also became the apostle Paul, and Paul became a new creation.

He was made fully alive.

The same can happen to you!

3

A Shoot from the Stump of Jesse

The Cross is a tree set on fire with invisible flame,
    that illuminates all the world.[1]
Thomas Traherne

"No, no, no life!"

These are the final and agonizing words of King Lear, the leading man of Shakespearean tragedy, when he realizes that his life is ebbing away.

By some measures, life has been good to Lear. He is the undisputed sovereign over a vast domain, the spoils of which can satisfy even his voracious appetite for glory. But Lear is also plagued by insecurity and his palace is riddled by intrigue, not the least by the schemes of his own children. Lear's eldest daughters, Gonerill and Regan, covet his fortune and plot to win his favor through flattery. The king, famished for love, devours their praise. He is blind, however, to the purer, more selfless love of a third daughter, the gentle Cordelia, who seeks only her father's best interests.

Predictably, the royal family implodes. At the end of the play, corpses litter the stage. Lear is convulsing in the corner, mortally struck by an assassin's blade. Gonerill and Regan lie together in a heap, the victims of lethal blows. Cordelia, mourning the loss of her beloved father, dies of a broken heart. The opportunist courtier, Edmund, though still alive, goes mad. Another attendant, Gloucester, is blinded, his eyes put out by the Duke of Cornwall.[2]

It is total carnage, one of the most appalling spectacles in theater.

Some regard *King Lear* as the outstanding achievement of the Bard of Stratford-upon-Avon. Others condemn it as brutal beyond redemption. In the mind of the famed nineteenth-century literary critic Charles Lamb, *King Lear* ought to be banned. It is "beyond all art . . . nothing but painful and disgusting."[3]

How can such a bloodbath be suitable for public consumption, let alone be esteemed as a masterpiece? Yet *King Lear* continues to dazzle audiences as much today as it did in the early seventeenth century.

How do we explain *Lear's* appeal?

Doubtless it is its insight into human nature. Almost every folly known to humanity is showcased in the drama. Happily, we, the audience, can watch from a distance as the pitfalls are borne by others, the actors on stage.

Yet in many ways, we don't escape the pitfalls. *Lear* is the dramatization of our own lives.

Even in the king's frantic last gasp—"No, no, no life!"— we hear a cry with which we can identify.[4] Fullness of life has eluded the king. So, too, it eludes us. Lear has a love-hate relationship with life, charmed by its possibilities and charred by its realities. So, too, do we. The king feels there must be more to life. So, too, do we.

The good news is that there *is* more to life.

There is a second tree.

The Greatest King

The Hebrew sage Isaiah heralded the second tree in a prophecy delivered around 700 BC:

> There shall come forth a shoot from the stump of Jesse,
>   and a branch from his roots shall bear fruit.
> And the Spirit of the LORD shall rest upon him,
>   the Spirit of wisdom and understanding,
>   the Spirit of counsel and might,
>   the Spirit of knowledge and the fear of the LORD.
>   (Isa. 11:1–2)

"A shoot from the stump of Jesse," "a branch from his roots"—this is the prediction of the second tree. But in this case, it is not a literal tree, with bark and twigs and leaves; rather, it is a person, the offspring of a man named Jesse, whose highly esteemed son, David, would become Israel's greatest king. And yet David was not the subject of Isaiah's prophecy, for he died long before Isaiah penned the words. A "shoot from the stump of Jesse" must refer to someone coming after David, a royal successor to David.

Whoever he is, he will be greater than King David. According to Isaiah, he will "bear fruit" and the fruit will bless entire nations. He will also possess supernatural insight and power. "The Spirit of the LORD shall rest upon him, the Spirit of wisdom and understanding, the Spirit of counsel and might, the Spirit of knowledge and the fear of the LORD" (Isa.11:2). He will exhibit the characteristics of God the Spirit, and will do so in a logical progression: wisdom will beget understanding; understanding will beget counsel; counsel will beget might; and might will beget the fear of the Lord.

A Positive Fear

It is especially the culminating attribute, the fear of the Lord, that distinguishes a Shoot from the Stump of Jesse. More than anything else, he will fear the Lord.

Normally fear is viewed as a negative emotion. It is dread in the face of something terrifying. Few gravitate to that kind of fear. But for a Shoot from the Stump of Jesse, the fear of the Lord is something positive. Far from mere trepidation, it is reverence for the One who holds in his hands the breath of life. Fearfully, the second tree will seek his life in the Lord.[5]

For this reason, he will "not judge by what his eyes see" (Isa. 11:3). Whereas Adam and Eve were captive to their eyes, attracted by the visual allure of the forbidden fruit, the second tree will not be so swayed. He will be resolute in his devotion to the Lord. He will seek his life in more *of*, never in more *than*, what God offers in himself.

This sort of fear is a pleasure to the second tree. "His delight shall be in the fear of the LORD" (Isa. 11:3).

Multitudes will take note: he will "stand as a signal for the peoples—of him shall the nations inquire, and his resting place shall be glorious" (Isa. 11:10). By his example, entire nations will be ushered into life.

A Beautiful Life

According to Isaiah, it will be a life unprecedented in terms of beauty. It will be full of comfort and free of hurt:

The wolf shall dwell with the lamb,
>and the leopard shall lie down with the young goat,
and the calf and the lion and the fattened calf together;
>and a little child shall lead them.
The cow and the bear shall graze;
>their young shall lie down together;
>and the lion shall eat straw like the ox.
The nursing child shall play over the hole of the cobra,
>and the weaned child shall put his hand on the
>>adder's den.
They shall not hurt or destroy
>in all my holy mountain;
for the earth shall be full of the knowledge of the LORD
>as the waters cover the sea. (Isa.11:6–9)

This is a breathtaking vision of life, almost too grand to take in. The wolf, a predator by nature, will dwell peacefully with the lamb. The lion, a carnivore, will become a grazer. A human mother, protective by instinct, will allow her baby to play over the hole of a cobra. No longer will nature be "red in tooth and claw."[6]

Life will be transformed.

Nothing will "hurt or destroy in all my holy mountain" (Isa. 11:9). There will be no pain, no sadness, no guilt. Loneliness, angst, and grief will vanish altogether. Wars will cease. Swords will be beaten into plowshares and spears into pruning hooks (Isa. 2:4; see Mic. 4:3–5). Peace, truth, and justice will be the new norm.

Paradise will be restored.

It is what we dream life should be, but what we think it can never be.

Having eluded us for thirty-five hundred years of recorded human history, how will this perfection of life materialize?

According to the prophet Isaiah, it will come through a Shoot from the Stump of Jesse.

To whom does this refer?

A Divine Man

Isaiah has already dropped several clues. The second tree will be a royal figure from the line of King David. He will bear the marks of God the Spirit. He will be guided by the fear of the Lord. He will save people from hurt and destruction. He will produce a harvest of spiritual fruit. He will bless entire nations.

Putting the clues together, a single candidate emerges. It is the itinerant preacher who walked the pebbled shores of Galilee in the days of the Caesars, the person known to history as Jesus.

The Lord Jesus Christ—he is the one heralded by Isaiah's vision. In fact, he amplifies the vision. New Testament authors are at pains to convey the full and exalted stature of Jesus.

"He is the radiance of the glory of God and the exact imprint of his nature" (Heb. 1:3).

"[He is] the image of the invisible God" (Col. 1:15).

"In him the whole fullness of deity dwells bodily" (Col. 2:9).

Jesus is both divine, the perfect image of God, and human, a revelation of God in mortal flesh.

Jesus the man embodies the life of God.

A Twist in the Story

Yet to see the earthly Jesus is to witness something seemingly less dignified and less divine. His life appears anything but full. Rather, it is plagued by tragedy. As Jesus himself acknowledged to the crowds of Caesarea Philippi, he is doomed to a calamitous demise.

"He began to teach them that the Son of Man must suffer many things and be rejected by the elders and the chief priests and the scribes and be killed" (Mark 8:31).

Jesus repeats himself, more vividly, on the road to Jerusalem.

"See, we are going up to Jerusalem, and the Son of Man will be delivered over to the chief priests and the scribes, and they will condemn him to death and deliver him over to the Gentiles. And they will mock him and spit on him, and flog him and kill him" (Mark 10:33–34).

This is a picture not of fullness of life, but of a life careening toward the most excruciating death of history, execution by crucifixion.

Death on a cross was an abomination. Hands and feet were pinned to wooden beams by iron spikes. When the upright beam was dropped into a hole, human flesh was torn and internal organs convulsed. Thus commenced a slow and excruciating death, in which the victim ultimately expired by asphyxiation. Too exhausted to push ankles against spikes, too weary to create space for lungs to expand, the crucified person suffocated from a collapsed diaphragm.

The first-century historian, Josephus, called crucifixion "the most wretched of deaths."[7] A contemporary of Josephus, the historian Tacitus, agreed: it is the "extreme penalty."[8] First-century philosophers Seneca and Cicero composed bleak epithets of crucifixion: "the criminal wood," "the most cruel penalty," and "that plague."[9]

In the ancient world, crucifixion was so reviled that the Greek word for cross, *stauros*, was considered an expletive and unfit for public conversation. Frequently in the literature, it was not even spelled out. Only the first letter, *sigma*, appeared, followed by six hyphens.

The cross was the most repugnant object of antiquity.

But it was also history's most fruitful tree. It was on a cross that a Shoot from the Stump of Jesse produced the world's greatest harvest. It was there that Jesus restored life to humanity.

Life drawn from an instrument of death—how is it possible? It is the quintessential paradox.

To understand its meaning, we must explore Jesus's own understanding of his death.

Pushing against the Tide

Jesus maintained that his death was *necessary*. He said he would *have* to suffer many things.[10]

Why?

Doubtless it was because Jesus opposed the present shape of the world. As we see in the first four books of the New Testament, he rejected the fallen condition of humanity. He waged war against disease. He cured blindness, paralysis, leprosy, hemorrhaging, mental illness, demonic possession, and the common cold. He fought against hunger, feeding the famished crowds. He stood against natural upheavals, calming violent storms. He even defied mortality, raising the dead.

Wherever Jesus went and whatever he did, he opposed what human life had become.

Perhaps most significantly, Jesus opposed sin, the malady at the root of every human ailment. He renounced sin singular—the attempt to build a life apart from God—and sins plural—the vices spawned by attempts to build a life apart from God.

Jesus bewailed the hypocrisy of religious leaders, the immorality of the Samaritan woman, the disloyalty of Peter, the avarice of Zacchaeus, the volatility of the crowds, the treachery of Judas, the duplicity of Thomas, and the timidity of Pilate.[11]

Sin singular and sins plural elicited stinging rebukes from Jesus. And it earned him no favor. By standing against the sins of people, Jesus pushed against the popular currents of the day, and that invited trouble.

Many times I have stood on a hill above a river in Canada and watched its volume surge inexorably to the Arctic Ocean. Never once have I witnessed even a single drop of its flow turn around and head upstream. Such a countercurrent would instantly be crushed by the dominant flow.

A similar crushing happened to Jesus. By swimming against the prevailing tide of his day, by pushing against the attempts of men and women to build better lives for themselves apart from God, by opposing the sins of humanity, Jesus ran headlong into the dominant flow. By pushing upstream, he elicited pushback.

A Mighty Collision

The logic of the pushback is clear. To his contemporaries, Jesus posed a mortal threat to the way they were pursuing their lives. In order to safeguard their existence they were forced to mount a counterattack. In self-defense, they pushed back. They sought to crush what would otherwise crush them and their way of life.

It was a battle to the death—the countercurrent of Jesus pushing upstream and the popular current of humanity pushing back. At the intersection of the two flows, a mighty collision took place.

It was the collision of a cross.

Thomas Traherne describes the wreckage of Jesus in crucifixion:

> Pale, withered, extended, tortured, soiled with blood, and sweat, and dust, dried, parched! O sad, O dismal spectacle! All his joints are dissolved, all his blood is shed, to

the last drop, all his moisture is consumed! What is here but a heap of desolations, a deformed carcase, a disfigured countenance! A mass of miseries and silence, footsteps of innumerable sufferings![12]

A Warrior with a Purpose

But the cross was more than the wreckage of a human body. There was a second reason why Jesus *had* to suffer—not only to absorb the blows of a threatened humanity, but also to mete out his own blows.

Jesus was no passive victim. He was a warrior with a purpose.

On the cross, Jesus did more than just die to life. He did more than expire by asphyxiation. He also died to sin.

"The death he died he died to sin" (Rom. 6:10).

That is to say, he defeated sin.

By going all the way to the end of his life without once yielding to sin, without once seeking to make a life for himself apart from God, without once succumbing to selfish ambitions, Jesus overcame sin.

For the first time in history, a man opposed sin all the way to the final breath. And by doing so, Jesus defanged sin.

He drained sin of its power. He reduced sin to a nonentity. He made sin nothing.[13]

An Agonizing Cry

It was not an easy victory. If any human would have been tempted to pursue an alternative course, it would have been Jesus. For the course appointed to him ran straight through the atrocity of a cross.

On a hill called Golgotha, Jesus faced the unimaginable. Beyond the physical agony, he endured estrangement from his heavenly Father. By absorbing human sin, he allowed a wedge to be driven into the heart of the Godhead, prompting history's most agonizing cry, "My God, my God, why have you forsaken me?" (Mark 15:34). It was a torment greater than the sum total of every other earthly torment.

For a human, the temptation to see another path—a more comfortable and pleasing path—would have been almost irresistible. Yet Jesus resisted.

It was a feat sufficient to spark incredulity on the part of the apostle Paul: "[He was] obedient to the point of death, even death on a cross!" (Phil. 2:8).

When at last Jesus shouted, "It is finished!" (John 19:30), he signaled completion of his mission. Never once did he succumb to sin. All the way to the end he resisted its appeal. At the very last, he vanquished its power.

Jesus died to sin.

And by doing so, he overcame what overcomes us.

A Shared Victory

Thus the cross of Christ was more than a victory for Christ alone. It was a shared victory. It was a triumph in which we, too, can participate. Because Jesus defeated sin, so, too, can we. We can die to sin and to its diminishment of our lives.

"[Jesus] died to sin, once for all . . . so [that we may] . . . consider [our]selves dead to sin" (Rom. 6:10–11).

In the folklore of the Canadian Rockies, the story is told of a shared victory between a park ranger named Felix Monroe and his loyal old mare. In the early spring, when Monroe was inspecting backcountry trails, he came upon the carcass of a deer. Dismounting, he began to poke at the remains with the barrel of his rifle. Suddenly, the calm was pierced by a bloodcurdling roar. It was the unmistakable growl of a grizzly bear, annoyed by the fact that someone was tampering with its supper.

The sow charged the ranger ferociously. Monroe managed to fire a shot into the torso of the bear, but it failed to stop her. With a terrific blow, the bear dashed away his gun and drove him to the ground, mauling him mercilessly.

At the instant Monroe was being dragged into the jaws of death, the faithful mare suddenly reared up and began attacking the bear. Lashing out with her forefeet and then, swinging around, striking also with her hind feet, the horse distracted the aggressor and drew its fury onto herself. The bear thrashed the horse's flanks and shredded her saddle to ribbons, and when at last finished with the rampage, she snorted in indignation and lumbered away.

The old mare was pitifully maimed. Slabs of flesh dangled from her shoulders and blood hemorrhaged from her side. Monroe, too, was gravely injured, but somehow managed to throw himself onto the back of the horse. Face down and soon unconscious, he was carried the many miles back to camp. When the two arrived, Monroe was still breathing, but the old mare, weakened by loss of blood, collapsed and died.

In the oral history of Canada, the horse is immortalized. She threw herself into a battle her partner could not win. She took the blows he could not survive. She gave her life so that he might keep his.

By dying to the bear, by refusing to yield to the bear's fury, the old mare liberated Monroe from its power. It was a shared victory.

A similar liberation takes place at the second tree. On the cross, Jesus took the worst that sin could mete out. He stood his ground. He resisted sin to the end. He purged sin of its power. He died to sin.

And we are the beneficiaries.

On the killing tree, he fought *our* battle, and his victory has become *our* victory. Dying, he set *us* free from the fury of sin.

"Behold, the Lamb of God, who takes away the sin of the world" (John 1:29).

An Undeserved Gift

Perhaps most remarkably, he died for us when we least deserved it.

"While we were still sinners, Christ died for us" (Rom. 5:8).

Whereas the courageous mare died for a devoted companion, Jesus died for rebels. It was while we were still sinning, while we were still seeking more in life *than* what we received from God, that he mounted the cross.

Our unworthiness makes his sacrifice all the more astonishing. In the words of Traherne:

> O Jesus . . . into what low abysses did You descend, in what depths of misery did You lie! Oh what confusions, what stripes and wounds, what desolations and deformities did You suffer for our sakes!

Then astonishment turns to adoration:

> In all the depths of Your humiliation I here adore You! It is sweeter to be with You in Your sufferings, than with princes on their Thrones, and more do I rejoice with You in Your misery, than in all their solemnities.[14]

To share in the fruit of Christ's sacrifice is to be filled with awe—the awe of being set free from the power of sin.

No Longer Slaves to Sin

Paul underscores the reality in a letter to the church of Colossae.

"If with Christ you died to the elemental spirits of the world, why, as if you were still alive in the world, do you submit to regulations—'Do not handle, Do not taste, Do not touch' (referring to things that all perish as they are used)? . . . But they are of no value in stopping the indulgence of the flesh" (Col. 2:20–23).

This is a typical Pauline sentence, overpacked with words and jumbled syntax. The apostle is attempting to compress a multitude of thoughts into a single breath.

He begins with the affirmation: "If with Christ you died."

At first blush, it is a puzzling affirmation. Surely only one person died on the cross, and it was not us. It was Jesus.

How can Paul write, "If with Christ *you* died"?

There can be only one answer: what happened to Jesus on the first Good Friday happened, in some sense, to us as well. It is *as though* we died with Jesus.

Paul explains the mutual death in the following way: "We know that our old self was crucified with [Christ] in order that the body of sin might be brought to nothing, so that we would no longer be enslaved to sin . . . for sin will have no dominion over [us]" (Rom. 6:6, 14).

It was "our old self" that died with Christ, specifically the old self in its attachment to sin. But now, because we have been crucified with Christ, we are "no longer . . . enslaved to sin." For the first time in our lives, we are no longer dominated by sin. We are able *not* to sin.

Set Free from Selfish Impulses

Paul identifies the sin which no longer binds us. We have died "to the elemental spirits of the world" (Col. 2:20).

Scholars have puzzled over the identity of the "elemental spirits of the world." To what do they refer? Most likely they refer to the "spirits" awakened at the foot of the first tree—in particular, the selfish desires which drive us to make a life for ourselves apart from God. It is certainly true that such desires typify humanity, that nothing in our "world" is more "elemental" than "spirits" of selfishness.[15]

To such "spirits" we have died.

Selfish impulses have not themselves died. They are still very much alive. It is we who have died to them.

Liberated from the selfish gene, we are no longer enslaved to self.[16]

Too few of us are aware of this liberation. Even many Christians struggle to come to grips with the meaning of co-crucifixion with Christ.

That is why Paul delivers a rebuke to his Colossian converts. "Why, as if you were still alive in the world, do you submit to regulations—'Do not handle, Do not taste, Do not touch?'" That is to say, why do you let yourself be dogmatized by the world?[17] Why do you allow your peers to determine what you handle, taste, and touch? Why do you yield to the social dogmas of the day regarding self-image, personal ambitions, and financial goals?

The Rot of Self-Serving Desires

The dogmas of the world won't take you very far. As Paul acknowledges, they will "perish as they are used." In other words, they will die in your hands.

My first exposure to death was an encounter with a rotten duck. I stumbled onto its dead body when I was four years old, walking alongside a lake in Los Angeles. Before my mother could whisk me away from the putrid sight, I managed to steal a glimpse at its maggot-infested gut. Instantly, I withdrew, taking two steps backwards. Even though just a young child, I knew instinctively not to touch the gruesome remains. I knew they would contaminate me.

As adults, we should be so discerning. Consider the things we touch every day: money, sex, and power. How we love to fasten our grip on these things. None of them is bad in itself—handled well, money, sex, and power can bring many blessings. But when we look to them for fullness of life, we are invariably disappointed. As inanimate objects, they are powerless to create life. To think otherwise is to watch them rot in our hands.

Hence Paul ventures a bold assertion. Money, sex, and power, and other earthly things like them, "are of no value in stopping the indulgence of the flesh." Here the word *flesh* is a synonym for selfish desires.[18] Pursuing money, sex, and power will not assuage selfish desires. It will not stop indulgence of the flesh. On the contrary, it will excite the flesh. It will exacerbate desires still further.

Evidence for this abounds.

Alexander the Great had immense power, conquering most of the civilized world, but when his troops were too exhausted to push into India, he broke down and wept.[19] Much power was not enough power. He wanted more.

Robert Louis Stevenson won fame as one of history's most beloved storytellers, writing such classics as *Treasure Island* and *Strange Case of Dr Jekyll and Mr Hyde*. But his last words, the self-composed epitaph of his tombstone, were doleful. "Here lies one who meant well, who tried a little, and failed much."[20] Much fame was not enough fame. He wanted more.

Claude Monet, impressionist painter par excellence, was downcast at the end. "I always wanted to believe that I would make headway and finally do something worthwhile. But, alas,

I must now bury that hope."[21] Much success was not enough success. He wanted more.

Most of us can identify with these disappointments. When we pursue material things as though our lives depended on them, none truly satisfies. Worse, each perishes in our hands, contaminates our lives, and excites the flesh still more.

Understanding Our Liberation

Happily, there is a better way. It is the liberation offered by Jesus. Through his death, he loosens the shackles of the flesh. He sets us free from selfishness and the self-serving dogmas of the world. He liberates us from the contaminating spirits of our day.

It is imperative to grasp the full significance of this liberation.

On the final night of July in 1834, eight hundred thousand slaves of the British Empire rose to celebrate their liberation. By a decree of Parliament, the night of their cruel bondage was coming to an end. In the words of famed historian George Trevelyan, at the strike of midnight an entire race of people climbed "onto the hilltops to watch the sun rise, bringing them freedom as its first rays struck the waters."[22]

For emancipated slaves, it was history's finest hour. To this day we celebrate the victory. Yet abolition did not put an end to the evils associated with slavery. The scourge of racism and social injustice remain with us today.[23]

While the victory was won, it was not fully implemented.

It is the same with our liberation from sin. What was accomplished on the cross of Christ was a full and final victory. Vanquished once and for all was the dominion of sin.

Dying with Christ, we are no longer *bound* to sin.

But the victory has not been fully implemented.

Christians—even Christians—still sin.

The apostle John cautions us against imagining otherwise. "If we say we have no sin, we deceive ourselves, and the truth is not in us" (1 John 1:8). Instead, we must acknowledge lingering sin, indeed, confront lingering sin. When we do, John invites us to a tree outside Jerusalem, the cross of Jesus Christ, where, in repentance, we can receive forgiveness of sins.[24]

"If we confess our sins, [Jesus] is faithful and just to forgive us our sins and to cleanse us from all unrighteousness" (1 John 1:9).

Lapsing into selfish thoughts and self-serving behavior is something we all do. But we are not bound to continue. We are free from the domination of sin. Cleansed and forgiven, we are able not to sin.

Seldom a day passes that I don't succumb to self-seeking desires. The allure of the elemental spirits is strong. I still pursue the imagined rewards of power, fame, pleasure, influence, and success as though they were the ultimate building blocks of my life.

Yet I am no longer enslaved to that pursuit. I am no longer dogmatized by it. Because of my co-crucifixion with Christ, I have come out from under its grip.[25]

"For freedom Christ has set us free; stand firm therefore, and do not submit again to a yoke of slavery" (Gal. 5:1).

Joined to Christ, I am no longer yoked to sin.

The Defeat of Death

Not only does Christ cut us loose from the shackles of sin, he also severs the cords of death.

According to Jesus, "Whoever believes in me, though he die, yet shall he live, and everyone who lives and believes in me shall never die" (John 11:25–26).

The truth is affirmed by John Owen in the title of his celebrated book, *The Death of Death in the Death of Christ.*

Thus the second tree grants a double blessing: freedom from sin's power and freedom from death's clutches.

Tolstoy underscores the two-fold blessing in a paraphrase of an old English fable. It is the account of a traveler who trips and falls into a disused well. On his way down, the hapless traveler seizes onto a branch protruding from a crevice in the well and clings to it with all his might, as though his life depended on it. For it does: lurking at the bottom of the well is a fire-breathing dragon ready to devour him the instant he loses his grip. Contemplating his plight, the traveler looks up and sees two mice, one black and one white, gnawing circles around his branch, reducing the branch to shreds and hastening his appointment with the dragon below. Just then, he also espies a few drops of honey oozing from the end of his branch and, impulsively, extends his tongue to lick up the sweet substance.[26]

For Tolstoy, the fable is an apt metaphor of life. We all cling to life as to a fraying branch, aware that the dragon of death awaits below. Hastening our fall is a white mouse and a black mouse—signifying day and night—gnawing away the minutes of our lives. In desperation, we reach out to any kind of sweetness that might distract us from our inevitable demise.

Life is but a quest for fleeting pleasure on the way to oblivion.

Except that it is not. In a Shoot from the Stump of Jesse, God creates a new way to be human. On the tree of Calvary, the Creator trades places with us, climbing, as it were, into our well and taking our place at the end of our branch, submitting himself to the death which ought to have been ours.

It is an act as exceptional as it is profound, and one worthy of the lyric composed by the hymn-writer Charles Wesley, "'Tis mystery all: th' Immortal dies: who can explore His strange design?"[27]

But the Immortal does more than succumb to the dragon of death. He also slays the dragon of death.

Note the encomiums of the apostle Paul, "O death, where is your victory? O death, where is your sting?" (1 Cor. 15:55). "Death is swallowed up in victory" (1 Cor. 15:54).[28] "If we have died with Christ, we believe that we will also live with him" (Rom. 6:8).

Hence to die with Christ is to celebrate a two-fold liberation: freedom from the dominion of sin and freedom from the scourge of death.

A Gracious Liberation

Perhaps most extraordinary of all, it is a freedom that costs us nothing.

"For by grace you have been saved through faith. And this is not your own doing; it is the *gift* of God" (Eph. 2:8).

But it is a freedom that costs God everything, even the death of his own Son.

"[He] did not spare his own Son but gave him up for us all" (Rom. 8:32).

An Enormous Love

How could a father give up his son?

I know I couldn't do it. In a moment of valor, I might sacrifice my own life to save another. But I could never sacrifice the life of one of our sons. I love them too much.

God, too, loves his Son, and with a love fiercer than that of any earthly father.

It is a love that actually predates time. According to the Son, "You loved me before the foundation of the world" (John 17:24). As an eternal love, it must also be an infinite love.

Endless in duration and unbounded in dimensions—this is
the measure of the Father's love for the Son.

There is no parallel.

Except that there is—the heavenly Father's love for *us*!

Willing to give up his own Son for us, God loves us with a love
comparable to that for his Son. Indeed, Jesus the Son, confirms as
much: "You . . . loved them *even as you loved me*" (John 17:23).

An Unconditional Love

To be the objects of infinite love implies that we are infinitely
lovely.

But we are not.

In God's eyes, we are actually unsightly. We have sought to
build lives for ourselves apart from him. We have jilted him. We
have committed spiritual adultery.

What could be more offensive? Far from lovely, we are ugly.

How, then, do we become objects of God's love?

To late-modern ears the question is vexing. We are a
performance-driven people. Whatever we possess, we must
earn, including especially love. Accordingly, we devote enormous time and energy to the pursuit of making ourselves attractive. The faces we paint, the bodies we sculpt, the images
we craft, the achievements we showcase—each is calculated to
win affection.

In other words, love must be earned.

But that puts us at odds with God. For his love cannot be
earned.

No mortal can earn infinite love.

But the inability to earn God's love doesn't stop God from
loving us. He allocates his love not on the basis of what we *do*,
but on the basis of who he *is*.

Regardless of our behavior, whether good or bad, he chooses to love us.[29]

A Father's Love

Why?

Because he is our Father and (good) fathers love their children.

"See what kind of love the Father has given to us, that we should be called children of God; and so we are" (1 John 3:1).

Fathers love without condition.

When I cradled each of our newborn sons in the maternity wings of their respective hospitals, I was overcome by wonder. My knees weakened and my eyes filled with tears. Instantly, I loved those boys. It was a love prompted not by anything they had done; after all, they had just been born, with time enough only to grimace, cry, and mess in their diapers, things hardly conducive to love. Nor were they especially attractive, with their scrunched up little faces.

Nevertheless, I loved them. Why? Because I was their father and fathers love their children.

So it is, even more wonderfully, with our heavenly Father.

"As a father shows compassion to his children, so the LORD shows compassion [to us]" (Ps. 103:13).

To put it another way, God's love is immutable.[30] It never varies. It is the pattern of our heavenly Parent to love his children, and the pattern never changes.

Unable to earn God's love, we are equally unable to lose it.

Not even a child who leaves his father for dead and squanders the family fortune on wild living can diminish the father's love. When such a child comes to his senses, turns around, and heads for home, he discovers a father who never took his eye off the horizon, waiting for just so much as the crest of the son's head to appear in the distance, ready to run to the son, embrace the son, and kiss the son, and to give the son his robe, his sandals, and his signet ring, and to throw a feast for the son.

"Let us eat and celebrate" (Luke 15:23).[31]

The heavenly Father loves even prodigal sons and daughters. Why?

Because (good) fathers love their children.

An Unexampled Love

Too many of us are unacquainted with unconditional love. We never learned love in that way. Perhaps early in life affection was withheld from us, discipline was harsh and unfair, and approval was difficult to win. Having never experienced unconditional love, even from the people closest to us, even from those who ought to have granted it most freely, we don't know how it feels or what it looks like. For this reason, many of us feel unworthy of God's love and imagine it beyond our reach.

But this can actually work to our advantage. Having dreamed of unconditional love most of our lives, we are quick to recognize it when it appears. And when it does appear, we welcome it with open arms. The good news of the free gift of God in Jesus Christ turns us around and points us toward home, where we fall into the arms of the heavenly Parent who has been scanning the horizon, awaiting just our return.

A few years ago, I was invited to lunch by a fellow pastor. He wanted to tell me about an important moment in his life. "After fifteen years of church ministry," he said, "I had a major heart change."

My curiosity was aroused, and I asked for the rest of the story.

It all started, replied the pastor, when a friend of his, another pastor, challenged him about his reserved personality. "You guard your heart too closely," observed the friend. "You have put up a wall and are hiding behind it. You don't let others in, and you don't give yourself out."

Initially, the pastor resisted the allegation. But the friend persisted, "You have put up a barrier and have shut yourself behind it."

To silence the friend, the pastor agreed to ponder the admonition and to pray about it.

At this point of the story, the man across the table from me put down his fork and looked at me with earnestness and exclaimed, "He was right. I had built a wall." Explaining further: "I have always been afraid of being left alone, and I withdraw for fear of rejection. Growing up, I felt rejected by my father. I was the eighth of nine children and the fifth and final boy. When I was little, my dad would go fishing with his buddies and I would walk with them down to the dock and watch from the shore as they motored out to the middle of the lake. From a distance, I could hear them laughing and having a good time. Sitting on the dock, all alone, I would cast my line into the water and sob."

At this point, I put down my fork. "How did your friend respond to your confession?"

A smile came to the pastor's face. "He said, 'Let's meet together every week for the next few months and study passages in the Bible about God's love. You need to discover the unconditional love of the heavenly Father.'"

And so they met, and in time the pastor discovered, in a way he never imagined possible, the unmerited and steadfast love of the Lord.

Soon the wall began to crack, and eventually it came down altogether. "When I saw how much God truly loved me, I was transformed. Not only was I assured of the presence of his love, but I also realized it was a love that I could never lose. I even dreamed that Jesus came to me and said, 'I'll go fishing with you . . . I'll always go fishing with you . . . I'll never stop going fishing with you.'"

The unconditional love of God—what explains such love?

Paul answers elsewhere in ten of the most beautiful words ever written—"because of the great love with which he loved us" (Eph. 2:4).

God loves us . . . simply because of his great love for us!

Overcoming Insecurity

Unfortunately, the unconditional love of God is one of Christianity's hidden gems. Like the pastor at the lunch table, many Christians don't feel or savor God's love.[32] And when they don't, they can't pass it on. And when they don't pass it on, the world remains ignorant of God's most appealing attribute, his unconditional love.

We must return again and again to the foot of the cross and gaze at the love hanging there. We must allow the love of the second tree to penetrate our innermost beings. We must pray it into our hearts. We must marvel that it is ours, and not because of anything we have done, but because of who God is. He is a Father who loves his children.

Touched by God's love, our walls will begin to collapse, just as they did for my pastor friend. When I asked the pastor's wife, who was sitting quietly at the table with us, whether she noticed a change in her husband, she became emotional. Tears rolled down her face and she nodded affirmatively. I then asked her how their three adult daughters had responded to the change of their father's heart. Gathering composure, she replied, "At first, they were cautious, not knowing what to think of this newfangled love. Then, seeing that it was genuine and not wanting to lose it, they became fearful. Finally, assured that the love was here to stay, they took every opportunity to spend time with their dad."

When we discover how much God loves us, we are set free from insecurities and can pass on the love to others.

Love for Today

In a dog-eat-dog world, unconditional love stands out like a radiant beacon in the darkest night. Fortunately, people don't have to queue up to wait for it. Two-step love—God's love to us and our love to others—is available today.

Years ago, an acquaintance of mine was hiking up a glacier when he lost his footing and fell into a crevasse. After hours of waiting for rescue, twenty feet down and wedged upside down in the ice, he was winched to the surface. Unfortunately, his body temperature had dropped so low that he sustained permanent brain damage. Today he limps around his municipality in a neon vest and plucks litter from gutters.

If only he hadn't been made to wait.

No one reading these words needs to wait. The second tree has borne its fruit. Freedom from bondage to sin and death is available today. The blessing of unconditional love can be ours immediately.

Help on the Way

We need only to cry out, "Help!"

"Help" is a cry of faith.

It is a confession that we can do nothing on our own to secure God's love. It is an acknowledgment that God does it all. It
is a willingness to join Christ on the cross, where he sets us free
from the selfish dogmas of the world and conquers the fleshly
impulse to make a better life for ourselves apart from him.

"Help me, Lord Jesus!"

To everyone who cries out these words comes rescue without delay.

"Now is the day of salvation" (2 Cor. 6:2).

My first experience of *King Lear* was an interpretation of
the play performed by the Royal Shakespeare Company. In the
last and pitiful scene, Lear cried out as though his life were no
longer worth living.

"I am a man as full of grief as age, wretched in both."[33]

"My soul is bound upon a wheel of fire that my own tears
do scald like molten lead."[34]

"I have a full cause of weeping."[35]

"No, no, no life!"[36]

With life ebbing away, Lear had nothing to celebrate.

It was a difficult sight to bear, the wretched king, and I
turned away in dismay.

Just then, the actor playing King Lear reeled around and
threw himself onto the only prop on an otherwise empty stage.
It was a frail and spindly tree, devoid of leaves. No more than
a few feet tall, it was an object so scrawny that it was embar-
rassing to watch a king commit his entire life to its withered
limbs.

In his final breath, Lear put his faith in a desolate tree.

From the producer of the play, it was a stroke of genius.

Life . . . in a desolate tree?

Yes!

We are called to throw ourselves onto a desolate cross. It may appear too feeble an object to bear the weight of our lives, but it is the only thing that can.

Trusting in the cross-work of Christ, dying with Christ to our sins, discovering in Christ the unconditional love of God—all of this awaits us at the second tree.

Yet remarkably, the second tree is only a prelude to something else.

Crucifixion with Christ is the right place to begin, but not the right place to finish. Having received the gift of unconditional love through death with Christ to sin, something else must take us forward.

We must move on to the third act of the drama, where we discover the fruit of a third tree.

4

The Tree of Life

God loves you with an infinite love,
  and does all that is possible for you,
and becomes by doing so your infinite treasure.[1]
Thomas Traherne

In 1905, at the same time as the Panama Canal was being dug
out of the isthmus of Central America, a channel of lesser dis-
tinction was being carved into the mountains of a remote outpost in the Pacific, on the Big Island of Hawaii. The channel
was called, inelegantly, the Kohala Ditch. To islanders it was
a gracious provision: capturing rain in the wet district of the
mountains, it distributed water to arid regions in the west, providing a lifeline to farmers and ranchers who might otherwise
have been ruined by drought.[2]

Six hundred Japanese laborers, using only pickaxes, shov-
els, and dynamite fashioned the twenty-three mile long con-
duit. Boring into volcanic hillsides, they constructed fifty-seven

tunnels. Negotiating gorges, they built numerous bridges. It was dangerous work, and it exacted a heavy toll. Seventeen workers lost their lives in as many months.

The sacrifices of a few brought hope to many. With water now streaming westward, the Kohala Ditch imparted life to an entire region.

A similar provision is made by the second tree. The sacrifice of one—Jesus Christ—rescued many from ruin.

But that is only part of the story.

Resurrection Life

By overcoming the scourge of the old life, Jesus actually created a vacuum. Where once stood the old life, now stands . . . what?

Having saved us *from* the power of sin, what has Jesus saved us *for*?

Many contemporary Christians are better schooled in the first half of Christ's work—death to the old life—than they are in the second half—birth to the new life.

Early Christians, however, were well-schooled in both. The crucifixion was central to their faith, but so, too, was the resurrection.[3] The fact that a man who was certifiably dead, wrapped tightly in burial cloths and sealed away in a sepulcher, was seen later walking among friends and strangers alike revolutionized their outlook. Early Christians greeted one another with the cry: "This Jesus God raised up" (Acts 2:32).

What made the resurrection of Jesus a transformational event was not just its newsworthiness—a corpse had been resuscitated—or its ramifications—mortality had been defeated—or its implications for the earthly Jesus—his teachings were vindicated. Each of these was significant, but something else was even more important.

The resurrection of Jesus Christ breathed *newness of life* into humanity.

When the stone was rolled away from the most famous tomb of history and when the carpenter of Galilee emerged from its dank interior, new life became a possibility on earth. The resurrected Jesus bore in his arms a new way to be human.

"Christ was raised from the dead . . . [that] we might walk in newness of life" (Rom. 6:4). Through the resurrection of Jesus Christ from the dead we can be born again to a living hope (see 1 Pet. 1:3).

By his resurrection, Jesus restored life to the fullness it had enjoyed in the garden of Eden.

Rightly, we honor the cross. It puts to death the old way of life. Equally, we celebrate the resurrection. It confers new life in place of the old.

According to the Bible, the two make a perfect whole. The cross anticipates the resurrection and the resurrection crowns the cross. To focus on one and not the other is to diminish the work of both.

Or to put it another way, the second tree carves a trail to the third tree.

A Heavenly Vision

The last of the three trees occupies a strategic place at both ends of Holy Scripture. It makes a cameo appearance in the initial pages of the Bible, in the garden of Eden, where it is given the name "the tree of life" (Gen. 2:9). Little more is said about the tree until it reappears at the end of the Bible in the book of Revelation.

The third tree thus bookends the Bible, which is appropriate, since by this tree God restores goodness to life.

If we are to discover how good life can be, we must acquaint ourselves with the Tree of Life.

It is a pity that we know this tree only slightly. Perhaps it is because of its distant location, far away in heaven, out of sight and out of mind.

Thankfully, the apostle John received special insight into the tree. By revelation, he was granted a vision of heaven, and what he saw there was so extraordinary that he had to use symbols to describe it.

A River Runs through It

According to John, "the angel showed me the river of the water of life, bright as crystal, flowing from the throne of God and of the Lamb" (Rev. 22:1).

A river runs through heaven, and it is "bright as crystal"— perfectly clear, immaculately pure, and superbly radiant. It is not only a bedazzling river, but it also emerges from an inexhaustible source, "from the throne of God and of the Lamb."

I am reminded of three great rivers in Canada: the Columbia, the Athabasca, and the North Saskatchewan. During the spring melt-off each of these rivers can expand to a hundred meters in girth. What generates such enormous flows? Remarkably, a single source: the Columbia Icefields, an amalgam of glaciers several hundred square kilometers in size and four hundred meters deep.

If these three rivers elicit awe, imagine how much awe is inspired by a river emanating from a source infinitely larger, whose headwaters spring from the throne room of God himself. The apostle John is wonderstruck.

He also reveals that the river is full of "the water of life." We might have expected it to be full of blood, emerging as it does from "the throne . . . of the Lamb." This is the same Lamb "who was slain" (Rev. 5:12; see 5:6), whose initial throne was a cross and whose blood was spilled for many. Jesus himself proclaimed the life-giving powers of his blood: "Whoever . . . drinks my blood has eternal life" (John 6:54). But the river of heaven does not contain blood. It is filled with water, and a very special kind of water—"the water of life."

By the blood of the cross, Jesus opened the door to life. By the water of heaven, Jesus sustains life.

A Torrent of Life

The apostle John discloses that the river runs down "the middle of the street of the city" (Rev. 22:2). Here the word *street* translates a Greek term which literally means "broad." Apparently, the river runs down the broadest avenue of heaven. That is a peculiar place for a river to run. Flooding the main street of heaven, where large numbers of people congregate, could cause many casualties.

Yet there are no casualties in heaven, only life, which is the purpose of the river and the reason why it runs down Central Avenue. God wants to inundate the citizens of heaven with everlasting refreshment, with "the water of life."

John also reveals something else about the river. "On either side of the river, [stands] the tree of life" (Rev. 22:2). At last, the third tree makes its grand entry. But it is an awkward entry. According to John, the tree stands "on either side of the river." How can a single tree bestride a massive waterway? Perhaps this is John's way of saying, figuratively, that both sides of the city are filled with emblems of life. If so, heaven is reminiscent of the garden of Eden, with its surplus of life-laden trees.

The Healing of Nations

Also resembling Eden, the trees are bursting with fruit, and especially the Tree of Life with "its twelve kinds of fruit, yielding . . . fruit each month" (Rev. 22:2). Unlike trees to which we are accustomed, each bearing a single kind of fruit and only once a year, the Tree of Life, nourished by springs from the throne of God, yields a variety of fruit and throughout the year. There is enough fruit in heaven to satisfy multitudes.

"The leaves of the tree were for the healing of the nations" (Rev. 22:2). We may recall that at the foot of the first tree there was no healing at all, only ailments of every kind. But beneath the branches of the third tree, there is supernatural balm from which every ethnicity receives healing.

It is immediately evident that, with the arrival of the Tree of Life, the vision of Isaiah receives its fulfillment:

> The wolf shall dwell with the lamb,
>   and the leopard shall lie down with the young goat,
> and the calf and the lion and the fattened calf together;
>   and a little child shall lead them. . . .
> They shall not hurt or destroy
>   in all my holy mountain. (Isa. 11:6, 9)

Likewise the prophecy of Micah:

> They shall beat their swords into plowshares,
>   and their spears into pruning hooks;
> nation shall not lift up sword against nation,
>   neither shall they learn war anymore.
>   (Mic. 4:3; see Joel 3:10)

In heaven, violence ceases, abuse stops, divorce ends, and anger dissipates.

"No longer will there be anything accursed" (Rev. 22:3).

No disease, no discouragement, no depression.

"[God] will wipe away every tear from their eyes, and death shall be no more, neither shall there be mourning, nor crying, nor pain anymore, for the former things have passed away" (Rev. 21:4).

The flaming sword that stood guard at the gate of Eden, debarring reentry, will be removed, and the river of the water of life will flood heaven with refreshment and satisfaction.

Life will be perfect.

The Face of Heaven

John sums up the vision in one sentence. "The throne of God and of the Lamb will be in it, and his servants will worship him" (Rev. 22:3).

One throne, two occupants. One deity, more than one person—God and the Lamb.

Servants of the Lord will drop to their knees and worship God. And their adoration will reach a crescendo when "they will see his face" (Rev. 22:4).

It was for this moment that the church father Augustine longed. With a fervent heart, he prayed, "Only let me see your face."[4]

What on earth we see only darkly, in heaven we shall behold with perfect clarity—the glory of God in the face of the Lamb, Jesus Christ.

No spectacle is its equal.

To see the glorified Jesus is to behold life, perfect life, fullness of life.

Climbing Upward

But—and perhaps here is the best news of all—we need not wait until heaven to behold such a sight. Like the apostle John, we, too, can steal a glimpse of the Celestial City. We can be renewed by the sight of the Tree of Life. We can experience fullness of life right now.

Wherever we are, we can begin a climb upward in which every step imparts increasing volumes of life.

Something like this happened on our honeymoon. When Lesli and I arrived on the island of Maui, we set our sights on a lofty climb. "Go to the top of Haleakelā for the sunrise!" was the advice of locals.

Haleakelā is an extinct volcano rising ten thousand feet above sea level. The summit is accessed by a narrow, thirty-eight-mile-long road, which wends its way up the mountain in a series of sharp switchbacks. To arrive by sunrise Lesli and I would have to leave our hotel room by four in the morning—not the sort of wake-up call favored by newlyweds! But we were determined. We wanted to experience the life of paradise to the full.

So on a chilly morning in June and at the end of a long drive, we beheld a most sublime spectacle. From high atop a volcanic ridge, we looked down at a sprawling crater seven-and-a-half miles long and two-and-a-half miles wide. When the sun rose, the upside-down cone morphed into a canvas of colors worthy of a master artist. Impressionistic yellows, creamy browns, and deep purples moved with the sun in geometric shapes across the valley floor. It was a primitive beauty, and our jaws dropped in wonder.[5]

Reflecting on his first visit to Haleakelā, the novelist Jack London wrote that it is "a workshop of nature still cluttered with the raw beginnings of world-making."[6]

Still today, Lesli and I reminisce about our trek to the top of the volcano. It was a life-imparting experience.

The higher we climbed the more alive we felt.

This is a maxim with which the apostle Paul could identify. For he also ascended to great heights. Having died with Christ, he also rose with Christ, and rose very high indeed. He encourages us to do the same, to rise as sharply upward with the resurrected Christ as we descended downward with the crucified Christ.

Paul urges us to climb high enough to look into heaven itself.

A Lofty Perspective

Here is how he puts it in his letter to the Colossians: "If then you have been raised with Christ, seek the things that are above" (Col. 3:1).

Grammatically, the "if" clause here represents a first-class condition, which means that its content is to be regarded as a *fait accompli*. It is as though Paul were saying, "*So then* you have been raised with Christ." And having been lifted up, you can now look into heaven itself. Indeed, Paul enjoins his readers to "seek the things that are above . . . set your minds on things that are above, not on things that are on earth" (Col. 3:1–2).

Things

Interestingly, the apostle chooses the nondescript word *things* to describe what is seen above. We might have expected him to point to the impressive ornaments of heaven, such as golden thrones and pearly gates. Instead, he highlights, somewhat colorlessly, the *things* of heaven.

Why *things*?

It is not because things are paramount in heaven. Things may be all-important on earth—things such as money, sex, and power—but they are not so above. In heaven, things are actually nothing in comparison to something else.

Paul identifies the main attraction of heaven. "Seek the things that are above, *where Christ is*" (Col. 3:1).

Heaven is "where Christ is."

Up above, Christ is the supreme focus, and Paul tells us why. We can summarize what he says in two words, each beginning with the letter *p*—posture and position.

Posture

According to Paul, the posture of Christ is significant. "Seek the things that are above, where Christ is, *seated*" (Col. 3:1).

To be seated is to be not standing.

Christ, as it were, is no longer on his feet, moving about and walking around. He is no longer healing the sick, teaching the disciples, multiplying the bread and the fish, rebuking the religious authorities, dying on a cross, or rising from the dead.

In Paul's vision of heaven, Jesus is sitting down, and it is important to understand why. It is because Christ has finished his work.

Position

This becomes clear when we notice *where* Christ is sitting, his position. He is sitting "*at the right hand of God*" (Col. 3:1). It's the highest position of all, reserved for the ranking dignitary of the universe. It is a seat Christ occupies by virtue of having finished his work. He has fulfilled the divine commission, the job the heavenly Father gave him to do.

It was the work of descending to a small planet at a distant corner of the universe in order to quash a rebellion of the planet's inhabitants, human beings, who were seeking to make a life for themselves, by themselves, apart from their Maker. It was a call to put right the things of earth.

And Christ did just that. By his death on a cross and his resurrection from the dead, Christ vanquished human sin. He fulfilled the divine commission and now sits at the right hand of God. From this lofty position he is surrounded by myriads of myriads and thousands of thousands of angels, who fall down at his feet and cry out, "Worthy is the Lamb who was slain, to receive power and wealth and wisdom and might and honor and glory and blessing" (Rev. 5:11–12).

Everything in heaven bows in worship of Christ (1 Cor. 15:27; Eph. 1:22).

To seek the *things* above is thus to fixate on a place where everything takes its cue from Christ, where everything is subservient to Christ, and where everything is sanctified by Christ. It is a place where nothing is wrong, nothing is diminished, and nothing is tainted.

Because of Christ, everything is perfect.

A New Reality

In other words, the things of heaven are not just different from the things of earth: they are the opposite. None of the things that bothered you when you woke up this morning or troubled you in your dreams last night or irritate you now as you move through the day can be found in heaven.

The criticisms of colleagues, the guilt of past mistakes, the insecurity of finances, the despair of loneliness, the pangs of illness—such things are nowhere to be found in heaven. Neither is partisan politics or international terrorism or sexual confusion or substance abuse or mental depression or domestic violence.

In heaven, Christ shapes *things* to perfection. In heaven every*thing* is replete with fullness of life.

For this reason, citizens of heaven are never tempted to build a life for themselves according to their own desires. It would be pointless. They already possess all the life they could ever want. They have life raised to the power of infinity!

To seek the *things* above is thus to celebrate a reality in which *things* could not possibly be better.

A Choice of Perspectives

The vision is inspiring. But we are earthbound creatures and still tied closely to a very different reality, where things are far from perfect and often downright ugly.

Yet according to Paul, we are not as earthbound as we may think. We have been raised up with Christ so high that we can look into heaven. With one foot still planted on earth, we can lift the other foot and stride, as it were, into the Celestial City. We can seek the *things* above. We can live now in the light of the reality of heaven.

This is a difficult concept to grasp. Especially when, opening the front door every morning, we step into a world reeling from less-than-perfect realities. But it's a truth we must grasp. For what Paul says here may be the most important piece of counsel he ever imparted to Christians.

He is calling us to look at things in a different way. He is saying earth's realities are not *ultimate* realities. Christians ought to know this. Having risen with Christ, we are able to look above the world's gloom and set our minds on heaven's glory. No longer controlled by the things below, we can take refuge in the things above.

That doesn't mean that we ignore earthly realities, treating them as though they didn't exist or weren't important. But neither does it mean that we allow those realities to determine our outlook and dictate our moods. As people raised with Christ, we can lift our eyes above the disappointments of earth and focus on the realities of heaven, "where all is well, and all is well, and all manner of thing is well."[7]

If it seems a bit of a stretch to live on earth in the light of heaven, consider this: you have done something like this many times before. Frequently, you live in the present in the light of realities still to come.

A few years ago, after spending a couple of weeks alone in a mountain cabin working on a book, I began to miss my family. I started counting the days until we would be reunited again, ticking them off one by one. With only two days left, I did something stupid. I backed the car into a tree stump, which produced a loud hissing sound, evidence of a tire going flat. There was a big gash in the sidewall of the tire. It was irreparable. To make matters worse, the nearest tire shop was over a hundred miles away.

By phone, I consulted a specialist and he told me that all four tires would need replacing, in order to insure even tread wear and to protect the shop from liability. He also revealed that the bill would total $950.

Normally, news of this sort would provoke a minidepression. But on this occasion, I was so preoccupied by the expectation of reuniting with Lesli and our boys that I hardly felt any discouragement at all. In fact, I sang along with Cold Play all the way to the tire shop, the entire hundred miles.

Overlooking today's disappointments in anticipation of tomorrow's prize is something we've all done.

When fog obscures the morning sun, we have a choice to make: either curse the gloom or set our sights on the afternoon burn-off. As Christians, we opt for the latter. We leave our overcoats in the closet and look forward to the warmth of the sun, which could arrive at any moment.

Indeed, a day is coming when the harsh realities of earth will be swallowed up by the perfect realities of heaven. In the blink of an eye, we shall inherit the *things* of heaven, forever. So why not live today in the light of tomorrow? Why not adjust our outlook and our moods to the realities above?

Practical Steps

To help us, Paul suggests two practical steps. First of all, he tells us to "*seek* the things that are above" (Col. 3:1); and, secondly, he encourages us to "*set [our] minds* on things that are above" (Col. 3:2).

Seek and set.

The two are different, but related.

You could say they resemble the two steps of operating the cruise control of a car. First, you seek the desired speed, and, secondly, you set—or lock into—that speed.

Paul is encouraging us to seek and to lock into the things above, which, as we know, is to seek and to lock into Jesus Christ. But note: it is not the Christ of the past, on the cross or in the resurrection, but the Christ of the present, seated at the right hand of God in heaven and presiding over ultimate realities. We lock into the ascended Christ.

Life in a Nutshell

Paul believes we are perfectly equipped to do so. "For [we] have died" (Col. 3:3)—died out from under the selfish impulses of the world and hence no longer bound to the things of earth. We are *free and able* to set our minds on things above.

We are also equipped in a second way: we have risen with Christ (Col. 3:1). Exactly what that means Paul now begins to unpack. He describes our coresurrection with Christ in eight words: "Your life is hidden with Christ in God" (Col. 3:3).

To simplify, let's remove temporarily the middle phrase, "hidden with Christ," and merge the first and the last terms. Five words remain: "Your life is . . . in God."

What is life *in God*?

Interpreting "In"

Much depends on how we interpret the little preposition "in." Grammatically speaking, it's a locative "in," specifying location. "Your life is . . . *located* in God."

To bring out the richness of the term, consider a similar phrase. "Your life is in California." As a native Californian, I can testify to what that means. Whoever locates *in California* experiences exactly what the brochures say: a life of sun, sand, and surf.

To be *in* California is thus to be immersed in the delights of the Golden State—so much so that those delights become a part of you. You could say that they indwell you. To be in California is to experience California within you.

So when Paul says, "Your life is . . . in God," he is also implying that God's life is in you. If you are in God, then God is in you.

Plugging In

Let's illustrate further by drawing an analogy from electricity. Every electrician carries a toolbox stuffed with plugs and sockets. And every electrician understands the relationship between plugs and sockets. When a plug is inserted into a socket, the plug gives nothing to the socket; instead, the socket gives everything to the plug. It sends a charge of electricity surging into the plug.

As Christians, we are the plug and God is the socket. To be in God is to plug into him. Not in the sense that we give anything to God, but in the sense that he gives everything to us. At the moment of our conversion, when by faith we entrust our lives to Jesus Christ, God sends a surge into us of what he essentially is, an electrifying current of his love and his peace and his joy and his righteousness—indeed, of his very own life. As Paul puts it elsewhere, we become "filled with all the fullness of God" (Eph. 3:19).

Filled with heaven's God, we possess a foretaste of the things above. So when Paul entreats us to set our minds on the things above, he is not uttering unintelligible gibberish. On the contrary, he is quickening our pulse. Having already sampled the things above, we yearn for precisely more of those things— more of heaven's love and peace and joy and righteousness, indeed, more of heaven's life.

Glory in Hiding

This book began with the question, What is so good about life? We have now received a striking answer: it is to be filled with the fullness of heaven's God.

How could life be better?

Yet there's a problem. Many people labor under the burden of felt-deficiencies. Even many Christians regard themselves as less than full, and especially of the things of heaven—love, joy, and peace. Christians can fret about personal losses, worry about broken relationships, and despair about potential illnesses, as though they were not very full at all.

Fortunately, Paul can sympathize. He himself endured a litany of disappointments.[8] Doubtless this explains the addition of the middle phrase of verse 3, which we temporarily omitted, "hidden with Christ."

"Your life is *hidden with Christ* in God" (Col. 3:3).

According to Paul, there is something about divine electricity that is not visible to the naked eye, that is hidden to people of our world. It certainly was hidden to people of the first century, when Christ walked the dusty lanes of Jerusalem. To his onlookers, he cut a miserable figure, antisocial and weak, worthy of public scorn, soon to be dispatched on a cross. "None of the rulers of this age understood [him], for if they had, they would not have crucified the Lord of glory" (1 Cor. 2:8).

But how can glory—especially the irradiating glory of God—be hidden to human eyes? The answer is simple: it is not because the glory is dim, but because its beholders are dim.

Dimness is a besetting human problem. And for Paul, some of the blame must be apportioned to "the god of this world," the devil, who "has blinded the minds of unbelievers" to "the glory of Christ" (2 Cor. 4:4).

To unenlightened minds, the radiance of Christ is obscure. So, too, is the radiance of Christians: their lives are "*hidden with Christ in God.*"

A New Day Dawning

But it won't remain hidden forever. "When Christ who is your life appears, then you also will appear with him in glory" (Col.3:4).

Mark it well . . . Christ will *appear*!

He will return to earth.

And when he does, what was hidden will become visible to all. Every eye will see and every knee will bow and every tongue will confess that Jesus Christ is Lord to the glory of God the Father (Phil. 2:10–11).

Or to put it another way, when on that day the face of Christ emerges from the shadows and every man, woman, and child beholds its brilliance, then all will acknowledge, "I get it! I finally get it! What was once obscure, I see fully!"

Beholding Jesus face to face and absorbing wave after electrifying wave of his sovereign power and infinite love and abiding peace and perfect righteousness and consummate joy will cause the things of earth to grow strangely dim and the riches of heaven to explode with overwhelming brightness.

When Christ returns, the reality of life in him will *appear* worth celebrating.

A Miraculous Indwelling

But for Christians, it appears worth celebrating now. Having risen with Christ, they already see the glory of Christ. It is a glory percolating in their hearts. At conversion, they received an infusion of the glory of divine life.

This is the "mystery hidden for ages and generations but now revealed to his saints" (Col. 1:26), a mystery which Paul can compress into three words: "*Christ in you*" (Col. 1:27).

The indwelling Christ is perhaps the capstone of Christianity. It is a reality which Paul underscores in nearly all of his letters.

"It is no longer I who live, but Christ who lives *in me*" (Gal. 2:20). The glory of God in the face of Jesus Christ has shone *in our hearts* (see 2 Cor. 4:6). "He who raised Christ Jesus from the dead will also give life to [our] mortal bodies through his Spirit who dwells *in [us]*" (Rom. 8:11). "Christ is [now] formed *in [us]*" (Gal. 4:19). "Christ is *in you*" (Rom. 8:10).

Hence, not only has Christ done something *to* us—forgiving our past sins and assuring our future in heaven—but he has also done something *in* us.

He has *in*-filled us with himself.

Paul urges us to reckon with this reality.

"Do you not realize this about yourselves, that Jesus Christ is *in you*?" (2 Cor. 13:5). "Do you not know that you are God's temple and that God's Spirit dwells *in you*?" (1 Cor. 3:16).[9]

A Well-Kept Secret

For too many people, it is an underappreciated reality. It may even be Christianity's best-kept secret.

When I was a boy, the neighbor at the end of the street pursued a unique hobby. He ranked the world's most beautiful lakes. I remember the day when he announced to my father that he had discovered a new Number 1. It was a lake far to the north and well off the beaten path. "Maligne Lake," he proclaimed, "is the world's best-kept secret."

As an adult, I visited Maligne Lake, and it is indeed a place of remarkable beauty. The color of its water is unlike that of other lakes—an ethereal aqua, the product of the rays of the sun hitting trillions of particles which, having been pulverized by glaciers, hang suspended in the water. In addition, the lake is framed by an elegant carpet of spruce, fir, and lodgepole pines, and sits at the foot of rugged peaks draped in glaciated ice. Healthy populations of grizzly bears, black bears, caribou, moose, mountain goats, and mountain sheep frequent its shores. The entire scene is spellbinding.

So awe-inspiring is Maligne Lake that we would have expected it to posses a long and storied history. But we would have been wrong. When the boundaries of Jasper National Park were drawn up in 1907, few people realized that within its confines was nestled a lake of such alluring charm. It was not until 1908, when an amateur explorer from Philadelphia by the name of Mary Schaeffer pushed far into the backcountry and discovered Maligne Lake, that its wonders were published to the outside world. Up to then, most were unaware of the treasure hidden in their midst.

Too often Christians draw up the boundaries of their identity without reference to the treasure within them. They are insensitive to the indwelling Christ.

If we understood fully the glory of Christ inhabiting our hearts, we would no longer entertain worries and fears. We would no longer dread earthly losses. We would no longer wilt under the opinions of people. We would no longer be anxious for tomorrow.

To know ourselves to be indwelled by Christ is to be filled by infinite life. It is to be secure in him. It is never to lose heart. It is always to be more than a conqueror.

A Fervent Prayer

This underappreciated reality gives rise to one of Paul's most passionate prayers. "I bow my knees before the Father [and pray] . . . that according to the riches of his glory he may grant you to be strengthened with power through his Spirit *in your inner being*, so that Christ may dwell *in your hearts* through faith" (Eph. 3:14–17).

Certainly Paul would pray the same for us today, asking God to make us cognizant of the Christ who dwells in our inner beings.

Paul finishes the prayer with an even more ardent plea. He begs God to give us "strength to comprehend with all the saints what is the breadth and length and height and depth, and to know the love of Christ that surpasses knowledge, that [we] may be filled with all the fullness of God" (Eph. 3:18–19).

He longs for us to comprehend the full dimensions of Christ's love—its breadth and length and height and depth—and to acknowledge the companion reality of the fullness of God's indwelling presence.

It is noteworthy that Paul prays for *strength* to comprehend, which implies that, left to ourselves, we lack strength to comprehend. Indeed, as we have seen, it is not easy to grasp the truth that we have died with Christ to sin, and hence to the impulse of making a life for ourselves apart from God, and that we have risen with Christ to newness of life, and hence to a place so high that we can look into heaven itself, where Christ is seated at the right hand of the Father, radiating a life that now indwells us.

Paul prays that we would be able to home in on Christ, and not just the Christ of the past, but also the Christ of the present, who effervesces the fullness of life in God.

A Great Exchange

How can we, as sinful beings, possibly deserve such an infilling? Having strayed from God, having sought to build lives for ourselves apart from him, how can we become suitable habitations of his glory?

Traherne acknowledges the dilemma: "Verily we are in danger of perishing eternally . . . [for] God cannot be reconciled to an ugly object."[10]

We need a good scrubbing. Sin clings to our inner beings like stage 4 cancer. It must be excised. We need the hands of a highly skilled surgeon.

Gratefully, we are attended by just such hands. The one who dwells in us is also the one who—prior to indwelling us—scrubs us clean.

Jesus is our surgeon. He has the power of God in his hands—hands working from a cross, hands paying the penalty of our sins.

Again, Traherne: "While God can never be reconciled to our sin, because sin itself is incapable of being altered, [God] may be reconciled to our person, because that may be restored."[11]

By grace, God can forgive "all our trespasses" (Col. 2:13). He can cancel "the record of debt that stood against us" (Col. 2:14). Through Jesus, who bore "our sins in his body on the tree" (1 Pet. 2:24), God can "set aside [our sins]" (Col. 2:14).

A few years ago, a friend of mine reported that he and his wife were struggling with their young daughter. She was defying them habitually. Recently, she even turned her back on them and walked away while they were attempting to address a disobedience. Her insolence broke their hearts and called for a firm response. They determined that, when the family sat down for a much anticipated Italian dinner that evening, the rebellious girl would be denied the customary fare. She would be served only a cup of soup.

When the hour arrived and the candles were lighted, when the place settings were prepared for antipasto and pizza, there was one exception. Where the daughter normally sat, there appeared only a small bowl with a single spoon.

When the girl saw the penalty of her sins, she burst into tears and ran around the table to her mother, crying, "Mommy, Mommy, I'm so sorry!" For a moment, all eyes fastened onto mother and child. With an expression both resolute and tender, the mother instructed the daughter to go back to her seat. After praying for the food, the mother looked intently into the eyes of the disobedient child and, smiling faintly, picked up her plate of antipasto and pizza and, walking to the other side of the table, placed it in front of her daughter. Then she picked up the bowl of soup and returned to her place.

Seeing this, the girl broke into even greater sobs of tears. She was undone by the sacrifice of a mother who would willingly take the place she deserved, absorbing the punishment which ought to have been hers.

A much greater exchange takes place between Christ and us. On the cross, Christ switches places with us. He takes the penalty we deserve and gives us the treasure we do not. He dies a death meant for us and in exchange clothes us with his righteousness.

In the words of Paul, "[God] made [Christ] to be sin who knew no sin, so that in him we might become the righteousness of God" (2 Cor. 5:21).

It is a righteousness that cleanses us from within and makes us suitable as vessels for a holy God.

It is history's most breathtaking exchange.[12]

It is a gift so stunning that it ought to fill the pages of Facebook, dominate the news of CNN, and go viral on YouTube.

But for God, it is enough that the gift fills us.

He wants to top us up with the Tree of Life with Its Twelve Kinds of Fruit.

It remains to discover exactly what the fruit entails, and what sort of life it imparts. To this we now turn.

The Tree of Life (with Its Twelve Kinds of Fruit)

An infinite Lord,
    who having all Riches, Honors, and Pleasures in His
        own hand,
is infinitely willing to give them unto me.
    This is the fairest idea that can be devised.[1]

Thomas Traherne

"Play it where it lies."

It is probably the most important rule in the game of golf.

Wherever a golf ball lands and rolls to a stop, there it must remain, untouched and undisturbed. It must be played where it lies.

There is, however, an exception to the rule. If a golf course becomes soggy, drenched by rain, mud can cling to the ball. Sticky appendages wreak havoc with the ball's flight, sending it off in all sorts of unwelcome trajectories, hooking into trees and slicing into lakes. Mud on a golf ball can turn an already challenging sport into a nightmare.

For this reason, *The Rules of Golf* make a provision for relief. It is called "lift, clean, and place." On muddy days, golfers can lift the ball from its resting place, clean it off with a towel, and then place it in an advantageous position. It is a merciful provision. Once clean, the ball flies longer and straighter.

We receive similar relief . . . courtesy of the three trees of the Bible.

In our examination of the Tree of the Knowledge of Good and Evil, we learned that we can become caked in the mud of our sins and disabled for the game of life. In our investigation of a Shoot from the Stump of Jesse, we discovered that we can be lifted from the mire of selfishness and washed clean. And in our encounter with the Tree of Life, we saw that we can be put back into play and flighted for maximum life.

We have yet to learn, however, what maximum life entails. On this matter, the apostle Paul is a reliable guide. In Colossians, he spells out the nature of that life. But he does so in a backwards manner, starting with what the life of God does *not* entail.

Life Is Not . . .

Paul begins with a directive: "Put to death . . . what is earthly in you" (Col. 3:5). Or more literally, "put to death . . . the members which are upon the earth." Here the word *members* refers to parts of the human body that can be used in earthly ways, in unwholesome ways, in ways which diminish human life. The apostle urges his readers not to misuse their bodies.

List No. 1

Paul provides a list of misuses. At the top of the list is "sexual immorality" (Col. 3:5). It refers to any kind of sexual interplay outside of marriage.[2] According to Paul, sexual immorality is something that must be put to death.

This may seem like an extreme directive, especially from a citizen of the Greco-Roman world of the first century, where sexual freedom was celebrated as an inalienable right. According to contemporary notions of sex, virtually anything was permissible, from multiple sexual partners to kinky indulgences.

Yet not for Paul.

Far from acquiescing to the practices of the day, the apostle places the misuse of sex at the top of his list of behavior detrimental to human life.

Rounding out the list is impurity (unclean thoughts), passion (uncontrolled yearnings), evil desire (illicit cravings), and covetousness (seeking what belongs to another). These, too, must be put to death.

It is noteworthy that underlying each of these behaviors is the impulse to grasp selfishly for oneself. In the case of sexual immorality, it is the impulse to gratify oneself in the body of another.

Happily, God intended sex to be gratifying, very gratifying.[3] The physical union between two people sparks a euphoria almost too sublime for words. In God's eyes, sex is special, so special that it must be governed by a formal contract.

Just as driving away from a car dealership in a new Ferrari, with the power of 660 horses exploding at one's feet, requires an official contract transferring title from the dealership to the new owner, so it is with sex. Just as it is "hands off" the steering wheel of a new Ferrari until the contract is signed, regardless of the inner desires to rev up the engines, so it is with sex.

But there is an important difference: sex requires not just a formal contract, but a public covenant.

It is the covenant of marriage.

When two people unite together in the covenant of marriage, they take formal title to each other. They belong to each other body and soul, which entitles them to ignite the engine of sexual gratification.

Sex is too valuable to be indulged in casually or recreationally. When two people are sexually active before taking title to each other, they tend to treat each other as rentals. When we rent a car, we do so for the convenience it affords: it delivers us to our destination quickly and safely. But we rarely wash or fine-tune a rental. We leave that to the rental companies, the owners of the car.

When, however, we purchase a car, we treat it differently. We provide for its upkeep, servicing and washing it thoroughly.

So it is with sex. When husbands and wives take ownership of each other through the covenant of marriage, they take special care of each other. What they own, they prize and protect. This is especially true in regard to sexual intercourse, where husbands and wives seek first not their own gratification but the pleasure of the other. They engage in sex for the good of their spouse. In this way, their lives are enriched.

Too often sex is decoupled from marriage. Flashed salaciously on screens, heated up in premarital trysts, or indulged secretly in extramarital affairs, sex devolves into a fever of self-grasping, which fails to edify the souls of participants. Far more rewarding is the self-giving sex of marriage.

In marriage, sex can be profoundly fulfilling. Outside of marriage, it can become a hollow gratification. No wonder sexual immorality heads Paul's list of destructive behavior. Instead of enhancing life, "the sexually immoral person sins against his [or her] own body" (1 Cor. 6:18).[4]

Paul ought to be applauded for standing up to the licentiousness of his day. Such boldness may heal many wounds.

Wrath and Grace

Human wounds elicit the wrath of God. "On account of these [that is, on account of the vices of Paul's list] the wrath of God is coming" (Col. 3:6).

But human wounds also elicit God's grace. They prompt a merciful God to provide for a way out, a new life, which is the gift of the third tree. Because of the resurrection of Christ, God can restore us to life.

We respond to this gift by rejecting the old ways and embracing the new. "In these [namely, in the old ways] you too once walked, when you were living in them. But now you must put them all away" (Col. 3:7–8).

List No. 2

In a second list, Paul adds to the destructive behaviors that must be put away: "Anger, wrath, malice, slander, and obscene talk from your mouth" (Col. 3:8).

Topping the list is the emotion of anger. Little eviscerates the human soul like anger, and especially the soul of the one who is angry. Even when aroused by legitimate grievances—such as rudeness or betrayal or disrespect or rejection—anger never embellishes life. It always diminishes it. When it is allowed to linger and fester, it can savage its owner, poisoning heart and mind. Not without reason, Paul abominates anger.

It is important to note that the items of the second list are propelled by the same impulse which governed items of the first list: the egocentric impulse to grasp for oneself. Anger, wrath, malice, slander, and obscene talk—each is prompted by the desire for selfish gain. Far from adding to life, each subtracts from life.

Dirty Fuel

To fall prey to the items of Paul's two lists is to fill up with dirty fuel.

Early in our marriage, after six years of living in England, Lesli and I mapped out a vacation across Europe. It was to be the "trip of a lifetime." We anticipated the joys of climbing mountains in Switzerland, meandering through museums in Italy, lying on beaches in France, canvassing ruins in Greece, and visiting Reformation sights in Germany.

No sooner had we crossed the English Channel, however, than our car broke down. Late on a Friday afternoon, the alternator went kaput. We were forced to spend the weekend in a disheveled hotel in the red-light district of Ghent, a city in Belgium, waiting for the repair shop to open on Monday.

When the car was finally mended, we set out again for the "trip of a lifetime." But in the lake district of northern Italy, again on a Friday afternoon, a key belt in the engine ruptured and we were forced to spend a second weekend waiting for mechanics to return for the workweek.

Gratefully, three days later, we recommenced the "trip of a lifetime." But while laboring up a steep grade in Greece, we sputtered to a stop. It was a Friday afternoon!

As we were towed to a gas station, we faced the prospect of passing another long weekend waiting for Monday morning. With monetary reserves now running low, we wondered if we might have to abandon the "trip of a lifetime."

When the Greek mechanic pulled his head out from under the hood, he exclaimed with satisfaction, "No problem here, you just got dirty fuel!" Evidently, somewhere back in Belgium we had filled up with tainted gas and it was the root of all our problems.

Fortunately, the remedy was simple. In the words of the lyrical mechanic, "You better drain the dirty fuel before it drains you!"

Dirty fuel—it can undermine the "trip of a lifetime."

God created each of us for the "trip of a lifetime." He made us for maximum life. Lovingly, he warns us to avoid dirty fuel.

That is why the apostle Paul gives us two lists of behaviors to be avoided scrupulously: sexual immorality, impurity, passion, evil desire, covetousness, anger, wrath, malice, slander, and obscene talk. Each of these amounts to dirty fuel, and each is ruinous to human life. We must put them to death before they put death to us.

Life Is . . .

Having showed us what the life of God does *not* entail, Paul now opens a window on what we have been anticipating ever since the beginning of this book—what fullness of life *does* entail.

Putting Off and Putting On

Paul starts by reiterating our identity in Christ. "You have put off the old self with its practices and have put on the new self" (Col. 3:9–10). Here the word *self* translates the Greek term *anthropos*, which literally means "man." According to Paul, we have put off the old man with his destructive practices.

The identity of the old man is no secret. We met him once before, at the foot of the first tree. His name is Adam.

Old man Adam, with his self-indulging practices—we have put him off. No longer do we mimic Adam. No longer do we seek to make a life for ourselves apart from God. No longer do we run on dirty fuel.

Instead, we "put on the new man," whose identity is also no secret. He is Adam's opposite. He is Jesus Christ.

As Christians, we put on Christ.

The verbal forms used here by Paul, "put off" and "put on," are terms borrowed from the textile industry of the day. They are clothing metaphors.

According to Paul, we take off old clothing and adorn ourselves with new. We strip away the self-grasping threads of Adam and slip into the radiant garments of Christ. In so doing, we make a striking fashion statement. We stand out as people who are "renewed in knowledge after the image of [our] creator" (Col. 3:10).

Imaging the Creator

This may seem like a puzzling way to describe the wardrobe of the Christian—"renewed in knowledge after the image of its creator"—but it contains an important insight. To put on Christ is to be clothed with a special kind of "knowledge," a knowledge which, when put into practice, images the Creator himself. When we put on the clothes of the new man Jesus Christ, we behave in ways that resemble God.

This confirms what we learned earlier. When Christ—the one in whom dwells all the fullness of God—comes to dwell in us, we exhibit in our behavior many of the attributes of our Creator.

In one of his most famous prayers, Jesus highlighted multiple in-fillings. "You, Father, are in me, and I in you, that they also may be in us. . . . I in them and you in me" (John 17:21, 23).

People who are in Christ—thus people in whom Christ dwells—are ahead of their time. They stand at the vanguard of something new and revolutionary. Their attire is cutting edge, *haute couture*, a sneak preview of the fashions of heaven. They are dressed to resemble God.

In Christ, humans receive a new face.

Changing Faces

In 2012, a man from Virginia received a new face. He was the beneficiary of the most elaborate face transplant in history. Twenty years earlier he had blown away the right side of his face in a hunting accident, terribly marring his appearance. Not surprisingly, he closeted himself away and on the rare occasion when he did venture into public, he put a bag over his head. As the years passed, his friends got jobs, married, and started families, but he remained a recluse.

Then he was put in touch with an innovative team of surgeons at the University of Maryland. Over the course of two long days, nearly twenty doctors fitted him with a new face. As soon as the anesthesia wore off, the man asked for a mirror. Looking at his new self, he gasped in astonishment, dropped the mirror, clutched the thigh of the lead surgeon at his bedside, and broke down in tears of joy.

He was a new man.

Not only did he feel an immense debt of gratitude to the medical team, but he was also thankful to the victim of an automobile accident whose face he was now wearing. He would never learn the identity of his benefactor. The parents of the donor requested anonymity.

As Christians, we, too, have new faces. We wear the likeness of one who died. Unlike the man with the new face, however, we know the identity of our benefactor. His name is Jesus.

Through a surgical procedure performed by God, the mangled face of Adam was cut away from us and attached to the crucified Christ, and the beautiful face of Jesus was cut away from him and transplanted to us.

We have been transformed from one polar extreme to the other. The gulf separating us from what we once were to what we now are is incomprehensibly wide.

Today, when we hold up a mirror, we do not see our old selves. We see a new person. We see a mirror-likeness of the Son of God, who is himself the perfect image of the heavenly Father.

To repeat Paul's words, we have been "renewed in knowledge after the image of [our] Creator."

All in All

What, exactly, do we see when we look at our new faces? How, in practice, are we mirror-representations of God?

Paul provides a clue.

"Here there is not Greek and Jew, circumcised and uncircumcised, barbarian, Scythian, slave, free" (Col. 3:11).

The face we now wear is not fixed by the typical social markers of our day. Ethnicity ("Greek and Jew"), religion ("circumcised and uncircumcised"), education ("barbarian, Scythian"), and socioeconomic status ("slave, free")—these are not the all-important characteristics of the Christian. Something else defines our identity. Actually, some*one* else does—Christ himself.

In his next words, Paul underscores our identity.

"Christ is all, and in all" (Col. 3:11).

In other words, Christ is *all* there ever was, is now, or ever will be. He is bigger than a universe 27.4 billion light-years in width and stronger than the collective energy of one billion trillion stars.

Christ is all.

And perhaps even more remarkably, Christ can be "in all."

As we have seen, when we plug into Christ, he surges into us. He fills us up with what he essentially is. He infuses us with his "all-ness." In terms of personal identity, we could not be more amply endowed.

"Christ is all, and in all."

This is a life-changing reality.

Inside of us flows the river of heaven itself, bright as a crystal, filled with the water of life, welling up from the throne of God and of the Lamb.

Inside of us grows the Tree of Life with Its Twelve Kinds of Fruit, yielding a bumper harvest year-round, putting an end to things accursed and bringing healing to the nations.

With the "all-ness" of Christ bubbling up within us, what feats might we perform! What power might we wield! What heights might we scale! What victories might we win!

No wonder Paul exclaims triumphantly, "I can do all things through [Christ] who strengthens me" (Phil. 4:13).

Indwelled by Christ, we cannot be defeated. We are indomitable, unassailable, invulnerable, invincible, and indestructible.[5] Consequently, we ought never to become discouraged. Just the opposite: filled by the "all-ness" of Jesus, "we are more than conquerors" (Rom. 8:37).

List No. 3

Still the question remains, What does the indwelling life of Christ look like in practice? According to Paul, it looks like the most splendid array of clothing ever modeled.

The first piece of clothing may be the most significant of all. Clothe yourselves, says Paul, with "compassionate hearts" (Col. 3:12).

Typically, the Greek word for "heart" is *kardia*. But here Paul uses the term *splanchna*, a word pointing to the deepest part of the human being, the very "bowels" of a person, like the bowels of a ship. At the core of our beings, we are adorned with compassion—with sympathy and mercy. From our depths, we radiate an empathy for others.

Not surprisingly, this piece of clothing featured prominently in the earthly life of Jesus. Seeing the multitudes stumbling along like sheep without a shepherd, Jesus had "compassion" on them (Mark 6:34). It is the same Greek word that tops Paul's list, *splanchna*, a deep-seated sympathy to the concerns of others.

Christians adorned by this item put others before themselves. They are motivated not by self-interest, but by the interests of others.

Rare in our day is the adornment of compassion. Driven by self-interest, late-modernity is self-focused. Welling up from its "bowels" is the impulse of selfishness.

Christian attire forms a stark contrast. It resists the elemental spirits of the world. Instead, it reaches out to others.

Paul also highlights other articles of clothing. In addition to compassion, the Christian puts on "kindness" (Col. 3:12)—

a generosity that knows no bounds, but is free-flowing and openhanded.

Furthermore, says Paul, put on "humility" (Col. 3:12). In Greek, the word is double-barreled: humble-mindedness. A humble-minded person defers not to him- or herself, but to others.

The fourth item of clothing is "meekness" (Col. 3:12), which means never being harsh, curt, or indifferent, but tender, sensitive, and soothing.

Fifth is "patience" (Col. 3:12), in particular, long-tempered and not short-tempered, regarding others not as impositions, interruptions, or distractions, but as worthy of uncomplaining attention.

"Bearing with one another" (Col. 3:13) is the act of dropping one's own life and picking up the life of another, hoisting the concerns of others onto one's own shoulders and treating them as one's own concerns.

Finally, "If one has a complaint against another, [forgive] each other" (Col. 3:13). At first, this item elicits a wry grin. Who *doesn't* harbor a complaint against another? Personal slights, injustices, betrayals, slanders, affronts, rejections, abuses, and many other expressions of ill-will assault us all. And when they do, it is natural to strike back, if not by inducing pain, at least by withdrawing affection.

However, as Christians, we "forgive each other." Here the Greek word is *charizomai*, which means "to give grace." When injured, Christians don't retaliate, but give grace. They don't repay in kind, but cancel outstanding debts. Rather than nurture resentment, they bestow blessings.

Forgiveness was a salient feature of the life of the earthly Jesus. If anyone had reason for bitterness, it was Jesus. He was the object of grave injustice—an innocent man condemned to an outlaw's cross—but he uttered scarcely a word of defiance. When he did speak, he spoke tenderly: "Father, forgive them, for they know not what they do" (Luke 23:34).

Paul urges us to do the same.

"As the Lord has forgiven you, so you also must forgive" (Col. 3:13).

Compassion, kindness, humility, meekness, patience, bearing with one another, and forgiving each other—these are the articles of the wardrobe of Christ, and also of people in whom Christ dwells.[6]

Pouring Out

The seven are the product of a single impulse—the desire to pour oneself into others for their good.

It is a revolutionary impulse.

It also represents a preliminary answer to the question, What does the life of Christ indwelling us look like in practice?

It looks like a life of outflow. Indeed, it looks like the life of the ultimate outflowing one, Jesus Christ, who came not to be served but to serve, whose every thought and deed was marked by compassion and kindness and humility and meekness and patience and forbearance and forgiveness.

For Christ, life was to give.

It is the same for those in whom Christ dwells. For Christians, *truly to live is fully to give.*

Life Is a Verb

We may sum it up this way: life, as God intended it, is a verb.

Life is an action. Life gives itself away.

This is a crucial insight, but an elusive one.

Few of us instinctively regard life as a verb. Rather, we view life as a noun, or as a collection of nouns. We define our lives in terms of people, places, and things—in terms of meeting people, visiting places, and accumulating things. We pursue life by pursuing nouns.

But this is to remain stuck at the first tree, propelled by the urge to seek life in more *than* what we have in God.

At the third tree, everything changes.

The Tree of Life opposes the elemental spirits of the world and rotates our understanding of life 180 degrees. No longer is life about grasping after people, places, and things. Rather, it is about blessing people, enhancing places, and giving away things.

Life is not about getting.

Life is about giving.

Happily, as Christians, we have a surplus out of which to give. We are recipients of the "all-ness" of Christ. We are filled by a treasure chest of his resources. We are equipped to pour ourselves into others.

This leads to a radical conclusion: *it is only by giving ourselves away that we begin truly to live.*

It may sound counterintuitive. Native impulses suggest that life ought to be constructed on the back of nouns, that life is its fullest when accompanied by an increasing array of people, places, and things.

But native impulses are wrong.

Nouns do not impart life. No amount of people, places, or things can ever satisfy the human heart. If we think they can, then we will watch them deteriorate in our hands and contaminate our lives.

Life—truly satisfying life—is a verb.

When I was a postgraduate student in Great Britain, I threw myself into the pursuit of a noun. Energetically, I studied for a PhD. Early on, things did not look good. After three and a half years of research, after the grind of trying to turn insights into prose, after supervisions in which only my mistakes were pointed out, the academic degree seemed to be slipping away. It was unnerving. I approached my study desk each morning in a cold sweat. I was curt with loved ones. I couldn't locate my smile. I was convinced that, without a PhD., my life would be diminished. The thought of losing this noun was unbearable.

Despair set in, as it often does at the prospect of losing nouns.

But as the research began to wind down, I made a life-altering discovery. In my times of Bible reading, I encountered a teaching that I had failed to assimilate. As a Christian, I was indwelled by Jesus Christ. I was topped up to the brim by the fullness of God himself. I could not possibly be more blessed than I already was. I was overflowing with the resources of my Maker: his love, his peace, his power, his goodness, his truth, and a hundred other manifestations of his life. Nothing in heaven or on earth could put a dent in the infinite fullness that was already mine, not even the loss of a shiny degree. As far as life was concerned, I could not be more full.

It was a liberating discovery. Not only did it ease the fears of failure, but it also freed me to invest in others—to spill out my fullness into my wife, my fellow students, my supervisor, and even a rowdy group of middle schoolers at church.

Too many of us run on empty. We navigate life on dirty fuel. You can see it on every street corner. You can see it in the comments section of every website. People are angry, overwhelmed, defeated, guilt-ridden, lonely, self-absorbed, and afraid of failure.

What they need is a new set of clothes, a new identity, a new face, a new way to be human. What they need is Jesus Christ.

Where do they find him?

He is found in those in whom he dwells. He is found wherever people showcase his wardrobe, radiating self-giving compassion, kindness, humility, meekness, patience, forbearance, and forgiveness. He is found wherever people pursue life as a verb and produce a portrait of the fullness of Christ.

A Portrait of Life

It is surprising where such portraits turn up. They can be discovered in the most common of places, sometimes right in front of our noses, sometimes even in our own homes.

When I was a teenager, my cousin Chris came to live with us. Ten years my senior, Chris was raised by a single mother who was mentally ill. She abused Chris as a child. In angry tirades, she would berate him until he had little option but to retreat into a world of fantasy. For hours, he would entertain "green genies from outer space" and "robots in flying saucers," his imaginary and only friends. In his late teens, Chris began to use hallucinogenic drugs, most likely to escape even further from the unpleasantness of his life. He also became incorrigible to the point of becoming a threat to people around him. For this reason, he was forcibly committed to a mental institution and the diagnosis was not encouraging: acute paranoid schizophrenia and an inability to cope with responsibility. Seven months later and much to our dismay he was released from in-patient care and thrust onto the streets of Tucson. From there, he bounced from one seedy hotel to another and frequently fell victim to violence and sexual predation.

Then one day Chris bought a Greyhound bus ticket to California. He had an uncle there whom he had not seen in years.

My dad took the call.

"Uncle Bill, it's Chris. I'm at a bus station in Del Mar. Could you come and pick me up?"

Shocked, my father and I sped off to retrieve a cousin I hardly knew, with whom we had lost contact, and who was arriving with only the tattered clothes on his back.

It was an unsettling reunion. Chris refused to make eye contact with us and turned instead to the wall and stared at the kitchen cupboard. When we attempted to comfort him by gently touching his shoulder, he would flail his arms and warn us that his associates, the genies and the robots, would come and take our scalps. After an hour or so of such balderdash, my normally decisive father turned to my mother and asked in bewilderment, "What should we do?"

Without hesitation, Mom replied, "We'll give him the loving home he never had."

Thus began a more than three-decade commitment to uphold a promise made one evening in a confused kitchen. Mom pledged to pour herself, mind and body, into this broken specimen of humanity, and it was a pledge she kept. She would feed Chris, clothe Chris, talk with Chris, listen to Chris's blather, clean up after Chris, and even scrub the messes around Chris's toilet. She would give Chris the maternal compassion he had never known.

Initially, Chris responded with indifference, sometimes with insolence, and occasionally even with physical threats, to the extent that we would fear for Mom's safety. But Mom never flinched. She gave to my cousin some of the best years of her life.

Mom was a Swedish beauty, her twinkling blue eyes and wavy blond hair turning heads well into her later years. She was a gifted woman, smart and sociable. She saw deeply into people's hearts and lifted their spirits. She might have assembled an impressive *curriculum vitae*, full of accomplishments and distinctions. She might even have founded a nonprofit or written a popular book.

But she wasn't interested in nouns.

For her, life was a verb.

She had a motto: "Drop things and pick up people."

This she did for Chris. She picked up her husband's nephew when he was a young man, a middle-aged man, and an older man.

Chris never became much, not by society's standards. He never held a consistent job. He made few friends. In time and assisted by medication, he was able to move out of our home and into a studio apartment. But he never went far.

Little of worldly significance came of Mom's investment in Chris. But there was an other-worldly consequence: the love she poured into Chris left a mark that would translate to eternal life.

A month after Mom died, Chris wrote me a letter and expressed what he had never expressed in person, indeed, what I thought him incapable of expressing.

"I wish to convey my sympathy at the passing of Betty. She gave so much to me. In my prayers, I am assured that Betty is in heaven. I rejoice that I, too, am assured of eternal life in Jesus Christ, and can look forward to seeing Betty again."

In Mom, Chris saw a portrait of the self-giving love of Jesus Christ. It was enough to draw him to saving faith in Christ and to lead him away from his tortured existence all the way to the perfections of heaven itself.

In my own home, I saw a portrait of fullness of life.

My dad watched gratefully as Mom attended to the damaged son of his sister, and he took every opportunity to praise her in front of the children. "I have never met anyone more like Christ than your mother!"

But it was not in Dad's nature to replicate such sacrificial service. He grew up in an advantaged home, with a butler and a maid. Even though he was a very loving father, he was accustomed to being served, not to serving.

Like many businessmen, Dad was a visionary. He was always one step ahead of the curve, anticipating trends and finalizing deals. Later in life, as his professional career wound down, he set his sights on becoming an author. He planned to write a commentary on the biblical book of Proverbs. He would also try to piece together his thoughts on how to be a success in the marketplace while, at the same time, maintaining a strong testimony for Christ. The remaining years would be devoted to advancing, in print, the work of the Lord.

It would be a retirement of nouns.

Then the unexpected happened.

The chemistry of Mom's brain began to change. Unusual for her, she began to experience bouts of depression, during which she would, even more unusually for her, blame my father for her despair. This was confusing to Dad. Could he really be the cause of her unhappiness? He resolved to find out. He asked God to show him new ways in which he could serve his wife. He throttled back on projects. He spent less time writing. He gave his time to attending to Mom.

As weeks rolled into months, Mom's despair did not go away. In fact, it worsened. Soon she was afflicted by another disorder—forgetfulness. On one particular afternoon, she steered her car in the wrong direction and wound up thirty miles from home and completely bewildered how she got there. Simple arithmetic began to escape her. Then the name of the president eluded her, then the name of her beautician, and finally even the names of her grandchildren. A visit to a neurologist confirmed our suspicions—she was suffering from the middle stages of Alzheimer's disease, early symptoms of which included depression and hostility to those closest to her.

Thus commenced a ten-year farewell, years which Dad had slated for writing, but which turned into anything but writing.

He changed seats with Mom, taking over the domestic duties, catering to her every need—making her meals, arranging her wardrobe, dressing her for outings, grooming her hair, cleaning up her spills, tucking her in at night, and waking up frequently to monitor her sleep. It must have been a trying time—a punctual man accustomed to hitting the pillow at the strike of ten now rising in the middle of the night to retrieve his beloved as she shuffled down the hallway "to help out those poor people down there." It must also have been difficult for this intellectual man, now forced to engage in conversations which seldom rose above the prattle of a child.

For years, Dad never left Mom's side, insisting that "I am the only one who knows how to take care of her."

In the last months of her life, Mom was remarkably free of despair. In fact, she became a new person, so content and full of joy that, in her simple ways, she made us long to be with her. She turned the dreaded "A" disease into a graceful way to exit this world.

What explains the transformation? From the anger of despair to the peace of contentment—how did it happen?

Medication certainly played a part. But to a family observing the changes and also to her medical team, something bigger was at play.

It was a verb.

Dad had poured himself into Mom. He put down his things and picked up hers. He made her things his things. He set aside ten years of his life—a decade he had planned out so carefully—and gave them to my mom.

To what end?

Well, no more books were written. Yet something else would be—a chapter in my mom's life that no doctor could.explain, an Alzheimer's patient at peace with herself and with her God.

The final chapter made an indelible impression on six grandchildren. When they gathered at the graveside, each spoke in turn of a man who had touched them deeply. Each delivered the same eulogy—the memory of a grandfather who emptied every last drop of himself into their grandmother.

This was the tribute that they gave at *his* graveside. A short three and a half months after the death of my mom, my dad stepped into eternity and joined hands again with the woman he loved.

No more books.

But life is more than books.

Life is more than nouns.

Sifting through my father's effects, I found on his nightstand a folded piece of paper. It was a letter I had written to him shortly after Mom died. It seems he kept it close to hand, reading it often.

Father's Day, 2011
Dear Dad,

I want to say again how grateful I am for the way you cared for Mom. As she declined mentally and was unable to care for herself, you presented her with a beautiful picture of Christ, putting your own goals on hold while attending compassionately to her. I cannot imagine how you could have served her better. As her son and yours, I thank you. From God's perspective, *it may have been your life's greatest accomplishment. . . .*

I am only disappointed that it cost you so much, the painful microfractures in your spine doubtless the result of the many times you had to lift Mom. . . .

No son could ever have a dad more loving, godly, prayerful, and more interested in his family than you. You are my friend and, together with Lesli, the best friend I've ever had.

I love you so much.

Happy Father's Day!

Tim

I'm glad I wrote the letter when I did. Any delay and it would have been too late. It sat on the nightstand a short eight weeks.

Name of the Verb

The apostle Paul has a final word to say about the nature of the life which indwells every Christian. It may be the most important word of all.

He gives a name to the verb.

"Above all these, put on *love*" (Col. 3:14).

It is a perfect one-word summary of the seven items of clothing on Paul's list. Compassion, kindness, humility, meekness, patience, forbearance, forgiveness—all of these are comprehended in the word *love*.

"God is love" (1 John 4:8).

When God dwells in us, he fills us with what he essentially is. He fills us with his love. Radical, supernatural, eternal, life-changing, self-giving love.

Paul yearns for us to comprehend the full scope of that love. In a prayer we have already encountered, he bares his heart: "I bow my knees before the Father . . . [and pray] that you, being rooted and grounded in love, may have strength to comprehend with all the saints what is the breadth and length and height and depth [of that love]" (Eph. 3:14, 17–18).

It is a prayer implying that we do not normally grasp the full dimensions of Christ's love. We need "strength" to comprehend.

In other words, we are weak. We too easily lose sight of the best thing in the universe: Christ and his indwelling love.

As Christians, we ought to know ourselves to be the most loved people in the world. Yet too often we imagine ourselves unloved. We are overtaken by worry, assaulted by anxiety, riddled by guilt, troubled by insecurities, alarmed by fears, broken by bitterness, withered by loneliness, and hounded by failures. We, the beloved ones, fall into the despair of the unloved.

If the well-taught converts of Paul in Ephesus could lose sight of their identity in Christ and become discouraged, how will we fare better?

Regular Reminder

It takes daily reminding that, as children of God, we are filled with a love so great that it can never be diminished—not by troubling circumstances, not by failed relationships, not by past regrets, not by present failures, not by any kind of loss. In fact, nothing in all creation can ever separate us from, nor deplete in the slightest, the love of Christ dwelling within us (Rom. 8:35–39).

Paul urges us "to know the love of Christ that surpasses knowledge" (Eph. 3:19). It is a beautiful paradox. How can we know what surpasses knowing? The words contain an implicit assurance—namely, that the love of Christ is so broad and long and high and deep that there will always be richer veins of it to mine.[7]

Paul calls us to dig deep and to grow in our understanding of that love, to be students of that love, above all to be students of the cross of Christ where that love reaches its most perfect expression. He urges us to meditate consistently on the crucified Christ, looking at him from every angle, in order to be swept up and consumed by torrents of his love.

Strategic Love

As we increase in the knowledge of Christ's love, we also increase in the capacity to reproduce that love. What is within us—the love of Christ—comes out of us, and touches the world in needy places.

The love of Christ is the world's most powerful shaping agent. It "binds everything together in perfect harmony" (Col. 3:14).

It pacifies hostile hearts. It heals dysfunctional families. It reconciles warring spouses. It brings together what is divided and binds in perfect union.

Only the love of Christ can produce such "perfect harmony."

This magnifies the role of contemporary Christians. As people in whom Christ dwells, we are medics to a sick world. We possess within us the balm to mend broken relationships and reform fractured societies. We possess the power to save the world.

It's not our power, but Christ's—the power of Christ working in and through us.

The world looks to us (whether it knows it or not) for a portrait of the healing love of Christ. We must not neglect the portrait. We must not trifle. We must distance ourselves from the bitter fruit of the first tree, with its self-grasping greed, and reject the elementary spirits of the world, refusing to make a life for ourselves apart from God. We must take off the tattered clothes of selfishness and die to sin.

And we must tarry at the second and the third trees—consuming their fruit, putting on new faces, pursuing life as a verb, imaging the self-giving love of Jesus, emptying ourselves into others for their benefit, and showcasing to the world the love that is found in Christ, which can dwell in them too.

Heaven's tree with its twelve kinds of fruit fills us to the brim with cruciform love—it is not only the most beautiful sight in the world, it is also the most needed.

In response to the question, What is so good about life? we have come to a breathtaking conclusion. Life is more glorious than anything the human mind could have conceived, when it is the life of God welling up in us in the form of the self-giving love of Jesus Christ. It is a life that could not possibly be bettered.[8]

Water for Parched Souls

When the first flurries of autumn carpet Hasting's Mesa in the San Juan Rocky Mountains of Colorado, two new colors are added to the palette of creation. The dusting of snow creates a blanket of white and the chill of autumn turns the leaves of aspens to yellow. These two colors—white and yellow—transform the landscape into a wonderland of beauty.

Every September, scores of photographers push their way into the high country to capture the mountains at the height of their glory. Tripods spring up everywhere and the best vantage points are staked out early.

When the photos are reproduced and shared with others at lower elevations, they spark amazement. Little enthralls the senses like the Rocky Mountains in the full flush of autumn.

If a light dusting of snow and the dying leaves of aspens can evoke such delight, just imagine what can happen with an outburst of the life of God.

In our weary world, the life of God is water to parched souls. And it is found in only one place, in people in whom Christ dwells.

That is the story of the three trees.

It can be your story too.

6

Trees in Bloom

O let me so long eye You,
 till I be turned into You,
and look upon me till You are formed in me,
 that I may be a mirror of Your brightness,
an habitation of Your love,
 and a temple of Your glory.[1]

Thomas Traherne

In the middle of a large wall in the Art Institute of Chicago hangs a small painting. It is a sixteen-by-thirteen-inch self-portrait of Vincent van Gogh. Twice I have stood in front of the canvas, and each time I have been chilled to the bone.

No matter from which angle I view the painting, whether from up close or from twenty feet away, whether from one side or from the other, I always feel as though van Gogh is looking right through me. His eyes—hollow, weary, and anguished—follow me wherever I go and bore into my heart. If the whole life of a person can be seen in the eyes, then van Gogh must have lived a tortured existence.

Indeed, as a young man, van Gogh was estranged from his father and married a prostitute. He took up painting but sold only one work during his lifetime, and that for a pittance. He suffered from severe depression and mental instability: two days before Christmas in 1888 he sliced off the lower lobe of his left ear and presented it as a gift at a brothel.

Van Gogh painted over thirty self-portraits. They were, I believe, his way of crying out for help.

In Gallery 241, the cry is palpable. Looking into his eyes, I feel him asking, "Why didn't you tell me?" A lump forms in my throat and blood rushes to my face. Then the question sharpens, "Why didn't you tell me about life . . . about how good life can be?"

A whisper forms on my lips, "Please forgive me. I am so sorry."

Suddenly the clamor of schoolchildren brings me to my senses, "How silly of me to be talking to a portrait 150 years old!"

No, not silly.

Today there are Vincent van Goghs all around us, hundreds of them, thousands of them, with weary souls and troubled hearts, people yearning for satisfaction in life but finding mostly disappointment. You can see it—you can always see it—in their eyes.

What do you say to people who have yet to discover fullness of life?

You tell them the truth. Jesus Christ promised life and promised it in abundance. Moreover, he has done everything in his matchless power to fulfill the promise.

On the cross, he purged the power of what ruins life—sin. On the cross, he paid the penalty of what ends life—death. In the resurrection, he opened the door to a new way to be human—fullness of life. In the combined work of the cross and the resurrection, he purified hearts and fitted them to be vessels of his life.

It is a life overbrimming with love, power, truth, peace, goodness, righteousness, comfort, and joy. And it can be yours when you put your trust in Christ, when you give as much as you know of yourself to as much as you know of him, when you venture your all on him.

When we give our lives to Christ, he gives his life to us. Better yet, he gives his life *in* us. When we become Christians, he fills us with himself.

Yet not all Christians know this abundance of life, and perhaps many reading these words feel less than full.

The problem boils down to this: you are probably unaware of your identity in Christ. You do not understand who you are in Christ and who Christ is in you.

The indwelling Christ—it's our blind spot as Christians.

Fortunately, there is a solution. There are several practical ways by which to remind ourselves of the life-changing riches we possess in Christ.

Focusing on Christ

It is essential to remember that we are the plug and Christ is the socket. When we put our faith in Christ, we plug into Christ and receive a surge of his life. Since nothing can ever unplug us from Christ—indeed, he promises never to leave us or forsake us[2]—nothing can ever stop the influx of his love and power and truth and peace and goodness and righteousness and comfort and joy.

Every day, we can stand in the current of Christ's life. Every day, we can reaffirm our position in Christ. Every day, we can seek, as Paul says, to "gain Christ" (Phil. 3:8).

In the words of first-century church father Ignatius, "Let what will come upon me, only so I may obtain Jesus Christ."[3]

For many Christians, there is often a less exalted goal. Rather than expend themselves to know Christ better, they tend to focus on their sins. They relive their shortfalls. They dissect past failures and analyze present transgressions. Such introspection may mesh comfortably with our self-absorbed culture, but it does not mesh well with God's Word. While much is said in the Bible about sin, about identifying and acknowledging sin, much is also said about putting sin in the rearview mirror. Prolonged contemplation of sin impedes forward movement. It is impossible to look backward and forward at the same time. "One thing I do," says the self-professed sinner named Paul, "[is to forget] what lies behind and [to strain] forward to what lies ahead" (Phil. 3:13–14).

What, then, do we do with sin?

We confess it, weep over it, repent of it—but we do not linger unnecessarily over it. For Paul, the length of time elapsing between acknowledging his sin—"Wretched man that I am! Who will deliver me from this body of death?"—and shifting into a higher gear—"Thanks be to God through Jesus Christ our Lord!" (Rom. 7:24–25)—is probably no more than a few seconds, since the two sentiments appear in consecutive sentences.[4]

We need a vision beyond self-analysis. And we have it in Jesus Christ. *He* is our vision. We become students of him.

Reading the Bible, we immerse ourselves in his teachings. Going to church, we worship with his people. Bowing for prayer, we stand in the flow of his life. Like Paul, we press on to know Christ better.

Discerning the Voices

Every day we receive a steady stream of verbal input. Some of it begins in our imagination—as interior dialogues of the mind—and some of it begins in the world—as the external messages of society. Too often it is burdensome input, focusing on life's problems and whispering negative words such as "You're going to fail," "You'll never be attractive," "You ought to be more successful by now," "You'll never escape the past," "You're destined to be alone," "You'll never amount to anything," "Your goals are beyond reach," "You'll never find happiness."

"You lost your job," "You're divorced," "You filed for bankruptcy," "You're hopeless."

"Shame on you!"

"You're not good enough!"

It is vital to discern the voices. Those stoking discouragement, fear, and guilt can be dismissed, because they do not fit the vocabulary of God. They do not originate from him.

To whom, then, do we owe dispiriting messages? The apostle Paul tells us. "We do not wrestle against flesh and blood, but against the rulers, against the authorities, against the cosmic powers over this present darkness, against the spiritual forces of evil in the heavenly places" (Eph. 6:12). The voice of discouragement belongs to the voice of darkness, hence to the devil. And the goal of Satan is to derail us, to slay us with negativity. He "prowls around like a roaring lion, seeking someone to devour" (1 Pet. 5:8).

As Christians, we must distinguish the voices. If they condemn us, they are not from God. "There is . . . no condemnation for those who are in Christ Jesus" (Rom. 8:1). If they are not from God, then they must be from the devil. And we do not need to listen to him. Indeed, we can rebuff Satan, the one who "disguises himself as an angel of light" (2 Cor. 11:14), for "[God] who is in [us] is greater than [Satan] who is in the world" (1 John 4:4). We can invoke a curse against Satan, telling him to go to hell, which is where he belongs.

We must attune ourselves to the voice of God, and especially to his promises.

God promises that "I will never leave you nor forsake you" (Heb. 13:5; see Josh. 1:5). We need not listen to the voice of loneliness, even when we feel desolate and deserted.

God promises that he will make us "more than conquerors through him who loved us" (Rom. 8:37). We must not listen to the voice of insecurity, even amidst apparent failure.

God promises that "all things work together for good, for those who are called according to his purpose" (Rom. 8:28). We need not listen to the voice of despair, even when facing trials.

God promises that we can "rejoice always" (1 Thess. 5:16; see Phil. 4:4). We need not listen to the voice of sorrow.

God promises "peace I leave with you" (John 14:27). We need not listen to the voice of doubt, apprehension, and vulnerability.

God promises that he has already "seated us with him in the heavenly places" (Eph. 2:6). We need not listen to the voice of anxiety, in regard to the future.

God promises that he will "graciously give us all things" (Rom. 8:32; see Matt. 6:33). We need not listen to the voice of want.

God promises that he "is for us" (Rom. 8:31). We need not listen to the voice of detractors.

God promises that he "will supply every need of [ours] according to his riches in glory" (Phil. 4:19). We need not listen to the voice of worry, even in times of loss.

When life-sapping messages assault us—and they do so with alarming frequency—we must consider the source. They do not emanate from the life-imparting God. Hence they can be discounted.

We must attune our ears to God. We must measure the voices against the promises of God.

Treasuring the Cross

The apostle Paul calls us to become students of Christ's love— "to know the love of Christ that surpasses knowledge" (Eph. 3:19). It is a love so vast that it cannot be fully apprehended. Far from discouraging us, this ought to prompt us to dip deeper into its inexhaustible riches.

Every day, we can position ourselves beneath the spigot of Christ's love. We can drink up its refreshment. We can learn more about its endless volume and affirm, along with Paul, that "the love of Christ controls us" (2 Cor. 5:14).

Countless things jockey for control of our lives—power, popularity, and pleasure. But only the love of Christ warrants that position.

To understand that love better we must meditate on the person of the crucified Christ.

"In his death is His love painted in most lively colours."[5]

"Greater love has no one than this, that someone lay down his life for his friends" (John 15:13).

"In this is love, not that we have loved God but that he loved us and sent his Son to be the propitiation for our sins" (1 John 4:10).

The self-sacrifice of Christ is history's greatest example of love.

Approach the cross regularly and attentively, leaving no cry unheard and no wound unseen. Explore the divine motive for the cross: "Because of the great love with which he loved us" (Eph. 2:4). Marvel at the divine grace of the cross: "God shows his love for us in that while we were still sinners, Christ died for us" (Rom. 5:8). Celebrate the divine infilling of the cross: "God's love has been poured into our hearts through the Holy Spirit who has been given to us" (Rom. 5:5). Revel in the remarkable consequence of the cross: that we are the most loved people in the world. And know that, as recipients of Christ's love, nothing can ever drive a wedge between us and that love—not public scorn, not cruel words, not bitter rejections, not painful tragedies, not unnerving failures, not even our own sin . . . nothing!

To know Christ loves us fully is to experience life to the full.

Stop tarnishing his love by assuming that it must be deserved. It has nothing to do with personal merit, which is a blessing, since none of us can ever merit it. Humble yourself and let the love of Christ sweep over you and remake you.

The love of Christ can overcome every deficiency.

It is our sufficiency.

It is our life force.[6]

Exhibiting Indwelling Love

When we become bearers of Christ's love, we become beacons of Christ's love.

When we experience Christ's love, we exhibit Christ's love.

Love cannot be held in. It is like a river in flood bursting its banks, like a pent-up geyser blowing its top. Love cascades out of the Christian and into the lives of others.

Earlier we met a pastor who, on discovering Christ's love for him, could no longer hide behind insecurities. He was set free to pour himself into the people closest to him—his wife, his daughters, and his church.

Much loved, he loved much.

The telltale sign of a growing understanding of Christ's love is an increasing output of Christ's love.[7] Indwelling love is authenticated by outward manifestations.

Hence we ought to ask ourselves, Are we expressing Christ's love to others? Do our lives look like verbs instead of collections of nouns? Are we gushing compassion, kindness, meekness, humility, patience, and forgiveness? Are we a force for unity in our divided world? Is our love a tonic to those around us?

It is often hard to answer these questions affirmatively. We tend to view ourselves in less commendable terms. But why?

We need to remember that Christ's love, which dwells in us, is an active love. It breathes new life into a dead world. It transforms those it touches. It turns sadness to joy, turmoil to peace, despair to hope, and loneliness to contentment.

Too often we fail to see the evidence of this love, even when it is right in front of us.

Whenever we put down a project in order to invest in others, whenever we credit a colleague with success instead of ascribing it to ourselves, whenever we rejoice in a classmate's acceptance to university instead of expressing resentment, whenever we resist talking about ourselves and listen to others instead, whenever we sympathize with the grief of another and feel his or her discomfort in our own hearts, whenever we respond to the misrepresentations of others by forgiving those who uttered them, whenever we give our money to the disadvantaged instead of nurturing our own fortune, whenever we risk ostracism by sharing the good news of God with others—whenever we do these things, we manifest the love of Christ.

Works of self-giving love in a self-grasping world are supernatural works. They are miracles. And they are symptomatic of the Christian life.

Learning from Suffering

In our technologically advanced society, we are vexed by suffering. It seems a cruel and unnecessary intrusion into an otherwise comfortable existence. It diminishes the luster of our lives. Or does it?

Frequently in history, the people who enjoy the most satisfaction are those who endure the most suffering.

Suffering is rewarding.

Listen to Fyodor Dostoevsky: "Pain and suffering are always inevitable for a large intelligence and a deep heart. The really great men are, in my view, always bound to feel a great sense of sadness during their time upon earth."[8]

Listen also to Leo Tolstoy: "It is by those who have suffered that the world has been advanced."[9]

More remarkably, listen to the apostle Paul, who is most alive when he is most afflicted: "I am content with weaknesses, insults, hardships, persecutions, and calamities. For when I am weak, then I am strong" (2 Cor. 12:10). He rejoices in suffering that resembles the suffering of Jesus. We are "always carrying in the body the death of Jesus, so that the life of Jesus may also be manifested in our bodies" (2 Cor. 4:10). It is by sharing in the dying of Jesus that Paul also shares in the resurrection life of Jesus.

Far from diminishing us, suffering enhances us.

Jesus, too, envisioned the benefits of suffering. He looked ahead to the pangs of the cross and regarded them as the "joy that was set before him" (Heb. 12:2) and "the hour . . . [when he would] be glorified" (John 12:23).

Fullness of life does not preclude suffering, but calls for it. As Christians, we should expect suffering, even welcome it.

On this point, the sport of surfing is illuminating. When the waves are large, upward of ten to fifteen feet, they can punish surfers. They produce massive wipeouts, driving surfers into a backwash of turbulent whitewater and pinning them down for many terrifying seconds. But when the big surf is ridden well, it produces moments of ecstasy. The key to riding big waves well is simple: surfers must learn from their wipeouts. Ecstasy comes through suffering.

It is the same for Christians.[10]

Practicing Thanksgiving

Paul calls us to give "thanks always and for everything to God the Father in the name of our Lord Jesus Christ" (Eph. 5:20). Elsewhere, he reiterates: "Give thanks in all circumstances; for this is the will of God in Christ Jesus for you" (1 Thess. 5:18).

There is genius in the instruction. Perpetual thanksgiving is a cure for discouragement. It is also a prescription for contentment. That is because it is impossible to be resentful and thankful at the same time, to grumble and give thanks simultaneously. Thankful people build antibodies to frustration, fear, guilt, worry, anger, and regret.

Tellingly, Paul calls us to give thanks *"for everything"* and *"in all circumstances."* By this, he does not mean for every *good* thing and in all *favorable* circumstances, for that would be superflous counsel. Instead, he encourages us to give thanks even for *disappointing* things and even in *troubling* circumstances.

During the most trying episodes of our lives, we must give thanks. Why? Because the promises of God are stronger than the most trying episodes—promises such as "all things work together for good" and nothing can ever "separate us from the love of God in Christ Jesus our Lord" (Rom. 8:28, 39), not even "tribulation, or distress, or persecution, or famine, or nakedness, or danger, or sword" (Rom. 8:35). With assurances like that, how can we ever despair? Rather, we can give thanks to God *in all things*.

Thanksgiving cuts through clouds of despair.

Begin and end every day with thanksgiving. Give thanks throughout the day. Discipline yourself to be thankful. When you do, you will rejoice in life.[11]

Remembering Fullness

It is easy to become a Christian. We don't do a thing. Through the death and resurrection of Jesus Christ, God does it all. We simply entrust ourselves to the saving work of Christ.

What is not easy is what comes next: remembering who we are in Christ. As we have seen, we are prone to forget our identity as Christians. It can escape us in an instant. The devil does not want us to remember, and he tempts us to adopt self-absorbed identities.

Paul provides an exercise by which we can lock into Christ. We have already discovered it. It is the discipline of seeking and of setting our minds on the things above. It is a process which must be repeated until it becomes automatic.

We must train our minds to view the things of heaven as our ultimate realities. We must rehearse over and over again the great truth that Christ, having completed his work, is now seated at the right hand of God. Consequently, the things of earth are waning realities, and present disappointments will soon be swallowed up by heaven's perfections. We can live today in the light of what is coming tomorrow.

We can dance *right now* into fullness of life, live *presently* as a verb, pour ourselves *immediately* into others, exhibit *without delay* acts of compassion, kindness, humility, meekness, patience, and forgiveness, and become *today* agents of change.

Setting our minds on the things of heaven is a daily challenge.

At times, it may seem like a tedious challenge, but tedium is not necessarily bad. Routinely, we wash our hands, eat our meals, and go to our places of work. Such routines, while tedious, are beneficial. But not as beneficial as locking into the realities of heaven.

Living presently in the light of what Christ has fashioned in heaven is not only possible, but exhilarating.

Remembering the Father's Love

Several years ago, my father asked me, "Tim, why don't you wear a wristwatch?" I answered him forthrightly, "I don't like wristwatches. They make my wrist itch. I don't know why anybody would wear them."

When my father died, he left a will in which he bequeathed one personal item each to my sister and me. To me he left . . . his wristwatch! When I read the fine print, I couldn't believe my eyes. My first thought was, "Really? I don't like wristwatches!" Quickly, however, I swallowed my words, for I remembered the moment when my father first asked me about wristwatches. I had answered him dismissively, effectively belittling his bequest. I could recall the expression on his face—it was one of puzzlement and disappointment. The memory makes me wince to this day.

That is not all. I also recollected the time when, several decades before, my father had purchased the wristwatch. It was after my graduation from high school, an event marked by a family vacation to Europe. My dad wanted to visit Switzerland, partly because of my desire to see storybook chalets clinging to alpine cliffs and partly because of his dream to purchase a Swiss-made wristwatch.

It was all coming back to me now—the moment when my father hovered over the store counter, interacted with the salesperson, tried to decide which model to buy, and even postponed the decision twenty-four hours in order to pray about it.

It was an important acquisition, not only for him, but also for me. As we left the shop, Dad turned to me and said, "One day this wristwatch will be yours!"

Way back then, my father was preparing for *my* future. He was setting things up for me. He wanted to give me something by which to remember him. In his mind, the perfect gift was a wristwatch. Every time I checked the time of day, by looking down at my wristwatch, I would remember him and the love which bound us together.

It was crushing to think that near the end of his life I had forgotten his loving intentions, and, even worse, had unwittingly brushed them aside. How I wished I could retract my words.

Our heavenly Father, too, has made a bequest, and with us in mind. It was a gift planned in eternity past and recorded in his will. It was the greatest benefaction of all—the gift of the death and the life of his only Son. The Father wants us to wear the gift, not on our wrists, but *in our hearts*.

It is heartbreaking to think that we might neglect such a gift. It is sobering to admit that we often spend vast segments of our lives—days, weeks, months, even years—without so much as glancing in the direction of Jesus Christ.

Surely it is time to amend our ways. We must strap on the Son, affixing him, as it were, to our wrists, so that throughout our daily lives we can look into his face and remember the Father's love.

Remembering the love of the heavenly Father—it's all we need for life.

Perhaps you are reading these words and feeling a gnawing restlessness in your heart. You are still searching for more in life.

The good news is that there *is* more. It can be found not in the things of this world, not in science or nature or possessions or money or religion or pleasure, but in Jesus Christ.

Nothing else will satisfy your heart.

In the three trees, we find what we are looking for, and far more.

Right now, my wristwatch is broken. So, too, is its wristband, cracked in several places. But even this Dad anticipated. In his will he made provision for repairs. "If the wristwatch breaks for any reason, send it to the authorized repair shop in New York City (see address below) and insure it for its full value. I will cover the costs."

Against every eventuality Dad arranged for us to stay connected.

It's true that we all break down at some point. "The world breaks everyone."[12] It may be through difficult circumstances or personal sins or lost friendships. Whatever the cause, brokenness is a constant of humanity.

No one understands this better than the heavenly Father. "He knows our frame; he remembers that we are dust" (Ps. 103:14; see Ps. 78:39). And he makes provision for breakdowns. He supplies an address where we can find repair.

It is the address of an orchard where stand three trees.

When you enter the orchard and walk among the trees, moving from the first tree to the second tree, and from the second tree to the third tree, you find healing.

You are repaired.

You advance along a trajectory that is consistently upward, rising to claim "the prize of the upward call of God in Christ Jesus" (Phil. 3:14).

Then you will know the answer to the question, What is so good about life?

In Christ, it could not be better.

Come into the orchard of the three trees.

Come often, come daily, and discover life . . . and discover life abundantly.

Notes

Chapter 1: Life, Cynics, and Three Trees

1. Thomas Traherne, *Centuries* (Oxford: Mobrays, 1960), 1.92. Traherne, whom I quote often, is a seventeenth-century English poet and clergyman. His meditations on life, *Centuries*, is lauded by C. S. Lewis as "almost the most beautiful book in English," in *They Stand Together: The Letters of C. S. Lewis to Arthur Greeves (1941–1963)*, ed. Walter Hooper (London: Collins, 1979), 492.

2. Alexandr Solzhenitsyn, *A World Split Apart: Commencement Address Delivered at Harvard University June 8, 1978* (New York: Harper & Row, 1978), 37.

3. Rare Earth, "I Just Want to Celebrate," track 4 on Rare Earth, *One World*, 1971.

4. Vincent van Gogh, "Letter from Vincent van Gogh to Theo van Gogh" in *Delphi Complete Works of Vincent van Gogh* (Hastings: Delphi Classics, 2014), 3–12, May 1882.

5. Van Gogh, *Complete Works*, 3–12, May 1882. Note also the reputed dying words of the great Russian author Leo Tolstoy: "To seek, always to seek," in *Leo Tolstoy*, ed. Harold Bloom (Broomall, UK: Chelsea House, 2002), 16.

6. In *The Selected Letters of Bertrand Russell: The Public Years: 1914–1970*, ed. Nicholas Griffin (London: Routledge, 2001), 85.

7. "Both Sides Now," track 5, side 2 on Joni Mitchell, *Clouds*, 1969.

8. For the influence of Christ on Western art, see cultural critic Malcolm Muggeridge: "Who could have foreseen . . . that the words of an obscure teacher in a remote outpost of the empire would provide the basis for a new and most glorious civilization . . . [and] would inspire the noblest thoughts [and] the most sublime art . . . the world has yet known," *Jesus Rediscovered* (New York: Doubleday, 1969), 82.

9. T. S. Eliot, "The Hollow Men," in *T. S. Eliot: Collected Poems, 1909–1962* (Orlando, FL: Harcourt Brace Jovanovich, 1991), 77.

10. The words of Ezra Pound, quoted by Peter Wilson, *A Preface to Ezra Pound*, canto 115 (London: Routledge, 2014), 188.

11. "The World I Know," track 3 on Collective Soul, *Collective Soul*, 1995.

12. This is the lament of Isabelle Eberhardt, daughter of Russian exiles in Switzerland, who spent much of her short life (dying at the age of twenty-seven) wandering in Northern Africa. See Caroline Moorehead, "What Is Nourished in Silence," *The Wall Street Journal*, May 25, 2012, https://www.wsj.com/articles/SB1000142405270 23034484045774079211124273882.

13. The words of Carlos Fuentes, author and leading Mexican intellectual, in Jose de Cordoba, "Author Was Mexico's Leading Intellectual Voice," *The Wall Street Journal*, May 15, 2012, https://www.wsj.com /articles/SB10001424052702303505504577406453974960164.

14. "We Gotta Get Out of This Place," on the Animals, *Animal Tracks*, 1965.

15. "Rock Bottom," track 14 on Eminem, *The Slim Shady LP*, 1999.

16. Peggy Noonan, *The Time of Our Lives: Collected Writings* (New York: Twelve Hachette Book Group, 2015), 186.

17. The assessment of author Henry James, quoted by James E. Miller, *Theory of Fiction: Henry James* (Nebraska: University of Nebraska Press, 1971), 292.

18. "Happy Ending," disc 2, track 13 on Tech N9ne, *Killer*, 2008.

19. The words of Clarence Darrow, in Ray Black, "Darrow Finds World Silly: Would 'Chuck It' If He Were 20," *The Pittsburgh Press*, February 1, 1933, 14.

20. See the chapter "Eternal Life Is the Supreme Good," in Augustine, *The City of God against the Pagans*, trans. Henry Bettenson (London: Penguin Classics, 2004), 14.4.

21. William Shakespeare, *Pericles, Prince of Tyre*, ed. Philip Edwards (London: Penguin Classics, 1995), 5.3.223–29.

22. *Centuries*, 4.9.

23. Johann Wolfgang von Goethe, *Egmont* (Charleston: Nabu Press, 2010), act 3, scene 2.

24. C. S. Lewis, *The Weight of Glory and Other Addresses*, ed. W. Hooper (New York: Simon and Schuster, 1996), 15–16.

25. Blaise Pascal, *Pensées*, trans. A. J. Krailsheimer (London: Penguin Books, 1968), 75.

26. See also C. S. Lewis: "This is a good world that has gone wrong, but still retains the *memory* of what it ought to have been," *The Complete*

C. S. *Lewis Signature Classics* (San Francisco: Harper, 2002), 32. Emphasis added.

27. Russell, *Selected Letters*, 85. Emphasis added. See also van Gogh: "I cannot do without something greater than I," in Sergey Markov, "Vincent van Gogh—One of History's Greatest Painters," *Genvive. com*, https://geniusrevive.com/en/vincent-van-gogh-one-of-historys-greatest-painters/.

28. Pascal, *Pensées*, 75.

29. According to Traherne, "God doth sovereignly and supremely desire both His own glory and man's happiness" (*Centuries*, 4.64). Moreover, in the words of Jonathan Edwards, "God's respect to the creature's good, and his respect to himself, is not a divided respect; but both are united in one, as the happiness of the creature . . . is the happiness in union with himself," in Edward Hickman, ed. "God's Chief End in Creation," in *The Works of Jonathan Edwards*, 2 vols. (London, 1834; repr. Edinburgh: Banner of Truth, 1979), 1:120.

30. See "Those who seek the LORD lack no good thing" (Ps. 34:10); "Bless the LORD . . . who satisfies you with good" (Ps. 103:2, 5); "He satisfies the longing soul, and the hungry soul he fills with good things" (Ps. 107:9); and "You open your hand; you satisfy the desire of every living thing" (Ps. 145:16). See also the teaching of Jesus in Matthew 5:6: "Blessed are those who hunger and thirst for righteousness, for they shall be satisfied."

31. See "Forestry Management Basics," published by the North Carolina Forestry Association, https://www.ncforestry.org/teachers/forest-management-basics.

Chapter 2: The Tree of the Knowledge of Good and Evil

1. Thomas Traherne, *Centuries* (Oxford: Mobrays, 1960), 1.75.

2. See Traherne: "[God] is not an Object of Terror, but Delight. To know Him therefore as He is, is to frame the most beautiful ideal in all Worlds," *Centuries*, 1.17.

3. As will become clear, the only thing God withholds from humans is the possibility of becoming like him (see Gen. 3:5).

4. John Owen, *Communion with the Triune God*, eds. Kelly M. Kapic and Justin Taylor (Wheaton, IL: Crossway, 2007), 128. Emphasis added.

5. On the matter of owing God an infinite love, see Jonathan Edwards: "We are surely under greater obligation to love a more lovely being, than a less lovely: and if a Being be infinitely lovely or worthy to be loved by us, then our obligations to love him, are infinitely great; and therefore, whatever is contrary to this love, has in it infinite iniquity, deformity, and unworthiness," Edward Hickman, ed. *The Works of*

Jonathan Edwards, 2 vols. (London, 1834; repr. Edinburgh: Banner of Truth, 1979), 1:298.

6. See also Psalm 97:9.

7. By providing an alternative to himself, God demonstrates love. See the allegory by Francine Rivers, *Redeeming Love* (New York: Multnomah, 1997), where the hero, Michael, proves his love for Angel by allowing her to search for love apart from him.

8. Fyodor Dostoevsky, *Crime and Punishment*, trans. David McDuff (New York: Penguin, 1991), 655.

9. "Your steadfast love, O LORD, extends to the heavens" (Ps. 36:5).

10. "The LORD is good; his steadfast love endures forever" (Ps. 100:5; see 1 Chron. 16:34; 2 Chron. 5:13); " I have loved you with an everlasting love" (Jer. 31:3).

11. "The LORD, the LORD, a God merciful and gracious, slow to anger, and abounding in steadfast love" (Ex. 34:6). This is the classic statement of divine love in the Hebrew Scriptures. See Numbers 14:18; 2 Chronicles 30:9; Nehemiah 9:17; Psalms 86:15; 103:8; 111:4; 112:4; 116:5; 145:8; Joel 2:13.

12. See the definition of love in 1 Corinthians 13:4–7, which is a picture not ultimately of human love, but of God's love, which we, as humans, are called to emulate (for this insight, I am indebted to my wife Lesli). "Love is patient and kind; love does not envy or boast; it is not arrogant or rude. It does not insist on its own way; it is not irritable or resentful; it does not rejoice in wrongdoing, but rejoices with the truth. Love bears all things, believes all things, hopes all things, endures all things."

13. Benedict de Spinoza, *The Ethics of Benedict de Spinoza* (New York: D. Van Nostrand, 1888), 193.

14. Fyodor Dostoevsky, *Notes from Underground* (Hamondsworth: Penguin, 1972), 34.

15. According to novelist and playwright D. H. Lawrence, "The real way of living is to answer to one's desires," *The New Morality*, eds. Arnold Lunn and Garth Lean (London: Blandford, 1964), January 17, 1913, letters 502–4, p. 80. Contemporary novelist Carol Edgarian writes, "The bully, the martyr, the lover and the thief are all driven by their desires. . . . Desire propels," "Driven by Desire," in *The Wall Street Journal*, June 2, 2012.

16. In John Gross, *The Oxford Book of Aphorisms* (Oxford: Oxford University Press, 1983), 33. See also the eighteenth-century man of letters Samuel Johnson, who asserts of the human, "When he has gained what he first wanted, he wants something else," *sermon* 12.

17. Quoted by Barry Morrow, *Yearning for More: What Our Yearnings Tell Us about God and Ourselves* (Carol Stream, IL: InterVarsity Press, 2010), 40.

18. Quoted by Walter C. Kaiser Jr., *What Does the Lord Require? A Guide for Preaching and Teaching Biblical Ethics* (Grand Rapids, MI: Baker Academic, 2009), 47.

19. Quoted by B. C. Forbes, *Finance, Business, and the Business of Life* (New York: B. C. Forbes, 1915), 317.

20. Persson on Twitter, quoted by Julie Bort in "The Man Who Sold Minecraft to Microsoft for $2.5 Billion Reveals the Empty Side of Success," in *Yahoo News*, August 29, 2015, http://finance.yahoo.com /news/ive-never-felt-more-isolated-153600734.html.

21. It is not just the wealthy whom money fails to satisfy, but people of every economic strata. In Great Britain, wealth has tripled across all spectrums in the past fifty years, but the percentage of "very happy" people has declined to 36 percent in 2005 from 52 percent in 1957. See Frederic Lenoir, *Happiness: A Philosopher's Guide* (New York: Melville House, 2016).

22. Quoted in Jonathan Abrams, "The Winter of Jerry West," *Grantland*, October 5, 2011, 1.

23. "Michael Phelps Says Rick Warren's Purpose Driven Life Saved Him from Suicide," Fox News website, http://www.foxnews.com/sports /2016/08/10/michael-phelps-says-rick-warrens-purpose-driven-life -saved-him-from-suicide.html.

24. Quoted by Walker Percy in *Lost in the Cosmos: The Last Self-Help Book* (London: Picador, 2000), chap. 18.

25. Mark Twain, *Tom Sawyer, Detective* (Mineola, NY: Dover Publications, 2002), 3.

26. See Pascal, *Pensées*, 75.

27. C. S. Lewis, *The Complete C. S. Lewis Signature Classics* (San Fransisco: Harper, 2002), 114.

28. *Centuries*, 3.59. Also Traherne: "It is of the nobility of man's soul that he is insatiable. For he hath a Benefactor so prone to give, that He delighteth in us for asking," *Centuries*, 1.22.

29. Desire is a winsome trait when it finds its object in God. Contrast the philosophers for whom desire is inherently evil. See, for example, Cicero: "It is insatiable desires which over-turn not only individual men, but whole families, and which even bring down the state. From desires there spring hatred, schisms, discords, seditions, and wars"; Plato: "The sole cause of wars and revolutions and battles is nothing other than the body and its desires"; and Lucian: "All the evils which come upon man—revolutions and wars,

stratagems and slaughters—spring from desire," in William Barclay, *The Letters of James and Peter* (Louisville, KY: Westminster John Knox, 1975), 114–15.

30. Noteworthy is the observation of Augustine: "O greedy men, what will satisfy you if God Himself will not?," *Essential Sermons* (New York: New City Press, 2007), 158.7.

31. See Augustine: "Whoever seeks to be more than he is becomes less, and while he aspires to be self-sufficing he retires from Him who is truly sufficient for him," *The City of God against the Pagans*, trans. Henry Bettenson (London: Penguin Classics, 2004),14.12.

32. An idea first coined not by the popular television series of the same name, but by the apostle Paul: "You were *dead* in the trespasses and sins in which you once *walked*" (Eph. 2:1–2).

33. See Augustine: "Pride is the beginning of sin. And what is pride but the craving for undue exaltation? And this is undue exaltation—when the soul abandons Him to whom it ought to cleave as its end, and becomes a kind of end to itself," *City of God*, 14.13.

34. For sin as an unacceptable affront to God, see Traherne: "To sin against infinite love, is to make oneself infinitely deformed: to be infinitely deformed, is to be infinitely odious in His eyes whose love of beauty is the hatred of deformity. . . . To be infinitely odious in His eyes who infinitely loved us, maketh us unavoidably miserable: because it bereaveth us of the end for which we were created which was to enjoy His love," *Centuries*, 2.4.

35. On the reluctance of God to express wrath, see Edwards: "God is often spoken of as exercising goodness and showing mercy, with delight, in a manner quite different, and opposite to that of his executing wrath. For the latter is spoken of as what God proceeds to with backwardness and reluctance, the misery of the creature being not agreeable to him *on its own* account," *The Works*, 1:114 (emphasis in original).

36. Accordingly George Steiner, *In Bluebird's Castle* (New Haven, CT: Yale University Press, 1974), 30.

37. From the film *Your Sister's Sister*, as quoted by film critic Joe Morgenstern in "'Sister's Sister': A Small, Vivid Gem," *The Wall Street Journal*, June 15, 2012.

38. Note Dostoevsky's critique: "There will be thousands . . . a hundred thousand sufferers who have taken upon themselves the curse of the knowledge of good and evil," *The Brothers Karamazov* (London: Macmillan, 2002), 259.

39. This is not to suggest that the only way to affirm satisfaction with God is by rejecting alternatives to God. In heaven, there will be no alternatives to God and we will affirm complete satisfaction there. For we shall

see him as he is, face to face (1 John 3:2), in unmasked glory, and it will be (so to speak) satisfaction at first *sight*. Here on earth, however, we express our satisfaction only by *faith*, a faith ventured both without a visual of God and in the presence of alternatives. By faith we opt to love God instead of something or someone else. When at last, however, the Lord *appears* and we *see* him in glory, we shall be insensible to alternatives. Doubtless satisfaction with God in heaven will be enhanced by our prior experience of evil on earth. Having lived under a veil of darkness, under the sin of opting for life apart from God, we will, when we *see* the glory of the heavenly Father and Son, experience raptures of satisfaction more profound than had we never encountered evil in the first place. Perhaps this explains (in another way) why God allows evil—"because it will bring us all to a far greater glory and joy than we would have had otherwise," Timothy Keller, *Walking with God through Pain and Suffering* (New York: Dutton, 2013), 117 (see also Keller's helpful discussion on pages 90–95). Note, too, Jonathan Edwards: "God wills to permit evil but only because that permission grows out of the ultimately loving and just will of God who can do no other than create what is ultimately the greatest good," *Works*, 1:397–402. Expanding on Edwards, see George Marsden: "The triune God had an essential disposition to communicate his love to other persons, so he created creatures whose purpose was to return his love yet who had the power to resist. That rebellious resistance led to an even higher expression of God's love as God the Son took on the guilt of sin and God's wrath and died for absolutely undeserving human rebels," in *Jonathan Edwards: A Life* (New Haven: Yale University Press, 2004), 488.

40. Traherne, *Centuries*, 1.78.
41. Leo Tolstoy, *A Confession and Other Religious Writings* (London: Penguin, 1987), 31.
42. Tolstoy, *Confession*, 31.
43. Tolstoy, *Confession*, 64.
44. Tolstoy, *Confession*, 65 (emphasis added).
45. Incidentally, those who allege intolerance are often guilty of intolerance themselves, especially when they dismiss biblical teachings out of hand.
46. See the implication of Philippians 3:7–8, where Paul, reflecting on his pre-Christian experience, regards early successes as "rubbish" compared to the "gain" he has now found in Christ.

Chapter 3: A Shoot from the Stump of Jesse
1. Thomas Traherne, *Centuries* (Oxford: Mobrays, 1960), 1.60.
2. William Shakespeare, *King Lear*, ed. G. K. Hunter (London: Penguin, 1972), 5.3.302.
3. Charles Lamb, *Critical Essays* (New York: Dutton, 1903), 32.

4. Note Lear's entire lament: "No, no, no life! Why should a dog, a horse, a rat have life, and thou no breath at all? Thou'lt come no more; never, never, never, never, never" (5.3.304–6).

5. In the psalter, "the fear of the Lord" is often regarded as a positive emotion, as *joyful* reverence before a God who dispenses fullness of life (see Pss. 25:14; 31:19; 33:8, 18–19; 34:11; 40:3; 47:1–2; 61:5b–6a; 86:11; 89:7; 102:15; 115:11; 147:11).

6. Alfred, Lord Tennyson, *In Memoriam*, ed. Erik Gray (London: W. W. Norton, 2002), canto 56.

7. Josephus, *Jewish Wars*, ed. H. St. John Thackeray (Cambridge: Harvard University Press, 1926), 7.23.

8. Tacitus, *Annals*, ed. W. Peterson (Cambridge: Harvard University Press, 1914), 15.44.

9. Seneca, *Letters*, ed. R. M. Gummere (Cambridge: Harvard University Press, 1925), 101.13–14; Cicero, *Verres*, trans. C. D. Yonge (Cambridge: Harvard University Press, 1903), 5.168, 162.

10. See Mark 8:31. The *necessity* of Jesus's suffering is repeated frequently in the Greek Scriptures. See Luke 24:26; John 12:34; and Acts 26:23.

11. See Matthew 5:20, 23:1–36, and Luke 11:47–48; John 4:3–19; Matthew 26:69–75; Luke 19:1–10; John 6:66–68; Matthew 26:14–16, 47–52, and John 13:21–27; John 20:24–29; Luke 23:1–4, 20–25; and John 19:14–16, 21, 38.

12. *Centuries*, 1.89.

13. According to Paul, "the body of sin . . . [is] brought to nothing" (Rom. 6:6).

14. *Centuries*, 1.89.

15. On translating the Greek term *stoicheia* as "rudimentary and worldly notions," hence as the selfish impulses fundamental to human beings, see C. F. D. Moule, *The Epistles to the Colossians and to Philemon* (Cambridge: Cambridge University Press, 1957), 90.

16. The key preposition in Colossians 2:20, *apo*, indicates escape "out from under" the selfish impulse; see N. T. Wright *Colossians and Philemon* (Leicester: Eerdmans, 1986), 125.

17. Translating the Greek term in verse 20, *dogmatizo*, literally, hence "to dogmatize."

18. Paul uses "the desires of the flesh" (Gal. 5:16) synonymously with "the lusts of the flesh" (see Eph. 2:3).

19. See Joshua J. Mark, "India and Mutiny," in "Alexander the Great," *Ancient History Encyclopedia*, November 14, 2013, http://www.ancient.eu/Alexander_the_Great/.

20. Robert Louis Stevenson, *The Complete Works of Robert Louis Stevenson*, ed. Alexander Japp (Hastings: Delphi, 2015), chap. 10, part 4.

21. Quoted by Ross King in *Mad Enchantment: Claude Monet and the Painting of the Water Lilies* (London: Bloomsbury, 2016), np.
22. G. M. Trevelyan, *British History in the Nineteenth Century and After: 1782–1919* (London: Penguin, 1965).
23. For the incomplete gains of the Civil War in America, see essayist Adam Gopnik: "Within a year of [Abraham] Lincoln's death, the great idea of Reconstruction was gone, and the re-subjugation of black Americans, with slaves turned into serfs, was begun through terror, not to end until well into the next century," *Angels and Ages: A Short Book about Darwin, Lincoln, and Modern Life* (New York: Vintage Books, 2009), 212–13.
24. On the importance of repentance, see the first of Martin Luther's ninety-five theses tacked onto the door of the Castle Church in Wittenberg: "When our Lord and Master Jesus Christ said, 'Repent' (Matthew 4:17), he willed the entire life of believers to be one of repentance."
25. For lingering sin in the lives of Christians, see Jonathan Edwards: "Allowances must be made for the natural temper, which conversion does not entirely eradicate: those sins which a man by his natural constitution was most inclined to before his conversion, he may be most apt to fall into still. Though grace, while imperfect, does not root out an evil natural temper, yet is of great power and efficacy to correct it," Edward Hickman, ed. *The Works of Jonathan Edwards*, 2 vols. (London, 1834; repr. Edinburgh: Banner of Truth, 1979), 1:302.
26. For the entire fable, see Leo Tolstoy, *A Confession and Other Religious Writings* (London: Penguin, 1987), 31–32.
27. From the hymn "And Can It Be That I Should Gain," in *Trinity Hymnal* (Great Commission Publications: Atlanta, 1990), 455.
28. Here Paul appears to be citing Isaiah 25:8. See also Hebrews 2:14–15, where the victory of the Son over death is a victory shared with God's other sons and daughters. "Since therefore the children share in flesh and blood, he himself likewise partook of the same things, that through death he might destroy the one who has the power of death, that is, the devil, and deliver all those who through fear of death were subject to lifelong slavery."
29. Dostoevsky celebrates the unconditional love of God: "A man cannot commit so great a sin as would exhaust God's boundless love. How could there be a sin that exceeds God's love? . . . Believe that God loves you so as you cannot conceive of it," in *The Brothers Karamazov* (London: Macmillan, 2002), 52. See also John Owen: "This God does upon the account of his own love, so full, so every way complete and absolute, that it will not allow him to complain of anything in them whom he loves, but he is silent on the account thereof,"

in *Communion with the Triune God*, eds. Kelly M. Kapic and Justin Taylor (Wheaton: Crossway, 2007), 115.

30. For the constancy of God's love, see John Owen: "Whom he loves, he loves unto the end. On whom he fixes his love, it is immutable; it does not grow to eternity, it is not diminished at any time. It is an eternal love, that had no beginning, that shall have no ending; that cannot be heightened by any act of ours, that cannot be lessened by anything in us," *Triune God*, 120.

31. For an excellent exposition of the story of the prodigal son, see Timothy Keller, *The Prodigal God: Recovering the Heart of the Christian Faith* (New York: Dutton, 2007).

32. See John Owen: "Christians walk oftentimes with exceedingly troubled hearts, concerning the thoughts of the Father toward them. . . . Few can carry up their hearts and minds to this height of faith, as to rest their souls in the love of the Father; they live below it, in the troublesome region of . . . fears, storms and clouds. . . . How to attain to this pitch [i.e., the heights of God's love for them] they know not. This is the will of God, that he may always be eyed as benign, kind, tender, loving, and unchangeable therein; and that peculiarly as the Father, as the great fountain and spring of all gracious communications and fruits of love," *Triune God*, 112.

33. *Lear*, 2.4.267–68.
34. *Lear*, 4.7.46–48.
35. *Lear*, 2.4.279.
36. *Lear*, 5.3.302. For more on Lear's futile search for fullness of life see 2.4.279–80: "This heart shall break into a hundred thousand flaws"; 3.4.303–4: "Unaccommodated man is no more but such a poor, bare, forked animal"; 4.1.10–12: "World, world, O world! But that thy strange mutations make us hate thee, life would not yield to old age"; 4.6.183–84: "When we are born we cry that we are come to this great stage of fools"; 4.6.194: "I am cut to the brains"; 5.2.3–4: "We are not the first who with best intentions incurred the worst"; 5.3.288.

Chapter 4: The Tree of Life

1. Thomas Traherne, *Centuries* (Oxford: Mobrays, 1960), 1.71; 2.25.
2. The rainfall gradient of North Kohala on the Big Island varies dramatically, ranging from one hundred and fifty inches a year in the mountains of the Honokane Valley to five inches on the arid coast near Kawaihae, two locations separated by a mere eleven miles.
3. As the apostle Paul confirms: "Christ Jesus is the one who died—*more than that*, who was raised" (Rom. 8:34).
4. Augustine, *The Confessions of St. Augustine*, trans. Edward B. Pusey (New York: P. F. Collier and Son, 1909), 1.5.5.

5. Upon seeing the sun rise at Haleakelā, Mark Twain called it "the most sublime spectacle I ever witnessed, and I think the memory of it will remain with me always," *Roughing It*, Project Gutenberg eBook (2006), chap. 76, https://www.gutenberg.org/files/3177/3177-h/3177-h.htm #linkch76.

6. Jack London, *An Autobiography of Jack London*, ed. Stephen Brennan (New York: Skyhorse, 2013), 217.

7. I have changed the tenses of this famous quotation of fourteenth-century Christian mystic Dame Julian from the future tense to the present tense, to underscore the present realities of heaven. Edmund G. Gardner, "Julian of Norwich," *The Catholic Encyclopedia* (New York: Robert Appleton, 1914).

8. For a catalog of Paul's suffering see 2 Corinthians 1:8–9; 4:8–9; 6:8–10; and especially 11:23–29.

9. See also 2 Corinthians 6:16 and Ephesians 2:21.

10. *Centuries*, 2.30.

11. *Centuries*, 2.30.

12. For the substitutionary nature of the death of Christ, see Romans 4:24–25: "Jesus our Lord . . . was delivered up for our trespasses"; and for a helpful exposition of this text, see Simon Gathercole, *Defending Substitution: An Essay on Atonement in Paul* (Grand Rapids, MI: Baker Academic, 2015), 73.

Chapter 5: The Tree of Life (with Its Twelve Kinds of Fruit)

1. Thomas Traherne, *Centuries* (Oxford: Mobrays, 1960), 1.17.

2. The word used by Paul in Greek is *porneia*, which in the first century was a catchall term for extramarital sex.

3. Of course, God also intended sex for procreation (see Gen. 1:28).

4. For the beauty and purpose of sex, see my book on marriage, especially the chapter "Fusing Bodies," Tim Savage, *No Ordinary Marriage: Together for God's Glory* (Wheaton, IL: Crossway, 2012), 105–19.

5. For the importance of the indwelling Christ, see John Calvin: "As long as Christ remains outside of us . . . all that he has suffered and done for the salvation of the human race remains useless and of no value to us. Therefore, to share in what he has received from the Father, he had to become ours and *to dwell within us* . . . for all that he possesses is nothing to us until we grow into one body with him," *Institutes of the Christian Religion*, ed. John T. McNeill, trans. Ford Lewis Battles (Philadelphia, Westminster, 1960), 3.1.1.

6. On the inward work of the Spirit of Christ see Jonathan Edwards: "The Spirit of God is given to the true saints to dwell in them, as his proper lasting abode; and to influence their hearts . . . as a divine supernatural spring of life and action. . . . He becomes there a principle or spring of

a new life. . . . So the saints are said to live by Christ living in them.
. . . Christ by his Spirit not only *is* in them, but *lives* in them; they live
by his life," Edward Hickman, ed. *The Works of Jonathan Edwards*,
2 vols. (London, 1834; repr. Edinburgh: Banner of Truth, 1979), 1:265.

7. For the four dimensions of Ephesians 3:18—"the breadth and length
and height and depth"—as the measurements specifically of Christ's
love see Harold W. Hoehner, *Ephesians: An Exegetical Commentary*
(Grand Rapids, MI: Baker Academic, 2002), 488.

8. It is a picture of life so good that Malcolm Muggeridge maintains that
he would "rather be wrong with St Francis of Assisi, St Augustine of
Hippo, and all the saints and mystics for two thousand years, not to
mention Dante, Michelangelo, Shakespeare, Milton, Pascal, than right
with [atheists] Bernard Shaw, H. G. Wells, Karl Marx, Nietzsche, the
Huxleys, Bertrand Russell and such like," *Confessions of a Twentieth-
Century Pilgrim* (San Fransisco: Harper and Row, 1988), 66.

Chapter 6: Trees in Bloom

1. Thomas Traherne, *Centuries* (Oxford: Mobrays, 1960), 1.87.

2. See the promise of Jesus in John 10:27–28: "My sheep hear my voice,
and I know them . . . and no one will snatch them out of my hand."

3. Jerome, "Lives of Illustrious Men," in *Theodoret, Jerome and Gen-
nadius, Rufinus*, vol. 3 of *The Nicene and Post-Nicene Fathers*, Series
2, eds. Philip Schaff and Henry Wace (Peabody, MA: Hendrickson,
1999), 367.

4. According to Paul, repentance is not intended to be a drawn-out af-
fair, but "only for a while" (2 Cor. 7:8), and forgiveness is to be
granted promptly, so as not to overwhelm the sinner by excessive
sorrow (2 Cor. 2:7).

5. Traherne, *Centuries*, 1.90. It is worth noting the entire quote: "In his
death is His love painted in most lively colours. God never showed
Himself more a God than when He appeared man; never gained more
glory than when He lost all glory; was never more sensible of our sad
state, than when He was bereaved of all sense. O let Your goodness
shine in me! I will love all, O Lord, by Your grace assisting as You do."

6. For an uplifting exposition of God's love see John Owen, *Communion
with the Triune God*, eds. Kelly M. Kapic and Justin Taylor (Wheaton:
Crossway, 2007), 105–32.

7. Thus Jesus affirms: "By this all people will know that you are my
disciples, if you have love for one another" (John 13:35); and see the
apostle John: "If God so loved us, we also ought to love one another"
(1 John 4:11).

8. *Crime and Punishment*, trans. David McDuff (New York: Penguin
Books, 1991), 315.

9. Quoted by George H. Guthrie in *2 Corinthians* (Grand Rapids, MI: Baker Academic, 2015).

10. For the paradox underlying the Christian life, see my book *Power through Weakness: Paul's Understanding of the Christian Ministry in 2 Corinthians*, Society for New Testament Studies Monograph Series 86 (Cambridge: Cambridge University Press, 1996), soon to be revised as *When I Am Weak, Then I Am Strong* (Wheaton, IL: Crossway).

11. On thanksgiving, see Traherne: "[God] can be delighted with thanksgivings, and is infinitely pleased with the emanations of our joy, because His works are esteemed and Himself is admired. What can be more acceptable to love than that it should be prized and magnified? Because therefore God is love, and His measure infinite, He infinitely desires to be admired" (*Centuries*, 3.82).

12. Ernest Hemingway, *A Farewell to Arms* (New York: Simon and Schuster, 1997), 226.

General Index

Scripture Index

Also Available from Tim Savage

"No one who reads this book will look at marriage in an ordinary way again."
KEVIN J. VANHOOZER, *Research Professor of Systematic Theology, Trinity Evangelical Divinity School*

"Embrace the message of this book and it will transform your marriage, your family, and your entire life."
COLIN S. SMITH, *Senior Pastor, The Orchard Evangelical Free Church*

For more information, visit **crossway.org**.